Building Strategy from the Middle

FOUNDATIONS FOR ORGANIZATIONAL SCIENCE
A Sage Publications Series

Series Editor

David Whetten, *Brigham Young University*

Editors

Peter J. Frost, *University of British Columbia*
Anne S. Huff, *University of Colorado* and *Cranfield University* (UK)
Benjamin Schneider, *University of Maryland*
M. Susan Taylor, *University of Maryland*
Andrew Van de Ven, *University of Minnesota*

The FOUNDATIONS FOR ORGANIZATIONAL SCIENCE series supports the development of students, faculty, and prospective organizational science professionals through the publication of texts authored by leading organizational scientists. Each volume provides a highly personal, hands-on introduction to a core topic or theory and challenges the reader to explore promising avenues for future theory development and empirical application.

Books in This Series

PUBLISHING IN THE ORGANIZATIONAL SCIENCES, 2nd Edition
Edited by L. L. Cummings and Peter J. Frost

SENSEMAKING IN ORGANIZATIONS
Karl E. Weick

INSTITUTIONS AND ORGANIZATIONS
W. Richard Scott

RHYTHMS OF ACADEMIC LIFE
Peter J. Frost and M. Susan Taylor

RESEARCHERS HOOKED ON TEACHING:
Noted Scholars Discuss the Synergies of Teaching and Research
Rae André and Peter J. Frost

THE PSYCHOLOGY OF DECISION MAKING: People in Organizations
Lee Roy Beach

ORGANIZATIONAL JUSTICE AND HUMAN RESOURCE MANAGEMENT
Robert Folger and Russell Cropanzano

RECRUITING EMPLOYEES: Individual and Organizational Perspectives
Alison E. Barber

ATTITUDES IN AND AROUND ORGANIZATIONS
Arthur P. Brief

IDENTITY IN ORGANIZATIONS: Building Theory Through Conversations
Edited by David Whetten and Paul Godfrey

PERSONNEL SELECTION: A Theoretical Approach
Neal Schmitt and David Chan

BUILDING STRATEGY FROM THE MIDDLE: Reconceptualizing Strategy Process
Steven W. Floyd and Bill Wooldridge

Steven W. Floyd
Bill Wooldridge

Building Strategy from the Middle
Reconceptualizing Strategy Process

Foundations for
Organizational
Science
A Sage Publications Series

Sage Publications, Inc.
International Educational and Professional Publisher
Thousand Oaks ▪ London ▪ New Delhi

For information:

Sage Publications, Inc.
2455 Teller Road
Thousand Oaks, California 91320
E-mail: order@sagepub.com

Sage Publications Ltd.
6 Bonhill Street
London EC2A 4PU
United Kingdom

Sage Publications India Pvt. Ltd.
M-32 Market
Greater Kailash I
New Delhi 110 048 India

Printed in the United States of America

Library of Congress Cataloging-in-Publication Data

Floyd, Steven W., 1950-
    Building strategy from the middle: Reconceptualizing strategy process /
by Steven W. Floyd and Bill Wooldridge.
        p. cm. — (Foundations for organizational science)
    Includes bibliographical references and index.
    ISBN 0-7619-0644-4 (cloth: acid-free paper)
    ISBN 0-7619-0645-2 (pbk. : acid-free paper)
    1. Strategic planning. 2. Middle managers. I. Wooldridge, Bill,
1954- II. Title. III. Series.
    HD30.28 .F578 2000
    658.4'012—dc21   99-050645

This book is printed on acid-free paper.

00   01   02   03   04   05   06   7   6   5   4   3   2   1

Acquisition Editor:	Marquita Flemming
Editorial Assistant:	MaryAnn Vail
Production Editor:	Sanford Robinson
Editorial Assistant:	Victoria Cheng
Typesetter:	Marion Warren
Indexer:	Molly Hall
Cover Designer:	Michelle Lee

Contents

PART II: NEW THEORETICAL HORIZONS: ORGANIZATIONAL KNOWLEDGE, SOCIAL NETWORKS, AND TRUST

Acknowledgments

Writing a book is an educational process, and there are so many teachers involved that it would be impossible to recognize all of them in a few words. Many of our intellectual mentors we have never met nor spoken to. We owe them a debt of gratitude that is only partially acknowledged by attributions in the text.

Doctoral students are a primary audience for this book, and our own students have played an important part in its development. Early in the process we used the outline and bibliography for the book to structure Ph.D. seminars at the University of Connecticut and the University of Massachusetts. Students in these seminars contributed ideas, source material, and constructive comments. We are grateful to David Baldridge, Kim Eddleston, Juan Florin, Sharon Foley, Tim Golden, Irene Houle, Kelley O'Neill, James McClain, Bob McDonald, Charles Park, and Kira Reed (at the University of Connecticut), and David Dudek, Jan Halvorsen, Andrew Watson, and Diana Wong (at the University of Massachusetts). In addition, Zeki Simsek at the University of Connecticut, and Hang Tran and Jim Pappas at the University of Massachusetts were especially helpful in offering critique and tracking down references. Avinash Mainkar, now of James Madison University and formerly a student at the University of Connecticut, has developed his own research from a middle-level perspective, and his conversations with Steve have contributed much.

The Management Department at the University of Connecticut qualifies as a place where doing good research is both rewarding and fun. In large part, this is due to the efforts of Jack Veiga who, as department head, has established a collegial culture that is populated by talented people. Steve's work has also been supported financially by the Ackerman Scholar's Fund at the School of Business Administration. At the University of Massachusetts, Bill received support from the Isenberg School's faculty summer research grant program.

We have been literally amazed at the level of support provided by the editorial board of the Foundations Series at Sage. Before we even started writing, the board pushed us to rethink our proposal and broaden our theoretical horizons. During the review process, we received many pages of thoughtful feedback from Dave Whetton and two anonymous reviewers. Anne Huff's help was truly immeasurable. It is difficult to imagine a more supportive and conscientious editor. She ably packaged her challenges to us in ways that pushed our ideas forward, and she significantly enhanced the quality of the final product.

While writing a book has many rewards, it takes time away from family. Our wives, Beverly and Linda, deserve special gratitude for their patience and willingness to tolerate marathon sessions of writing and revision. And to Jenna and Andrew, Bill finally has the answer they want to their question, "Is the book finished yet, Dad? "

Finally, we would be remiss not to acknowledge the many professionals and organizations who have cooperated with our research. They have given generously of their time, and their wisdom has been invaluable. Like any developing theory, however, the ideas presented here must withstand the critical scrutiny of experts in the field and ultimately empirical validation. To this end, we present what follows as a work in progress. We take responsibility for its inevitable flaws and look forward with excitement to the field's continuing development of mid-level strategy process research.

SWF
WRW
Amherst, Massachusetts

To Boots and Ray, whose contribution lies behind every word
—SWF

For my first and best teacher, Dorothy Hall Wooldridge, 1925–1999
—BW

Introduction: Rationale and Timing of the Book

The knowledge and social influence processes at the middle play a key role in determining the organization's capacity to innovate and renew its capabilities.

In the time since the strategic management field emerged as an academic discipline roughly 30 years ago, the nature of competition among firms has changed markedly. For much of this period, competitive conditions and relationships among firms remained relatively stable over significant periods of time. Today, however, ever-changing technologies, new products, and evolving market preferences have created a climate in which little is stable. Rather than positioning themselves among known competitors, firms today must continually re-create their futures, their bases of competitive advantage.

Paralleling this shift, for much of its history, the academic literature in strategy has focused on the actions and decisions of top managers. Indeed, the field has often been defined by its focus on the problems and issues facing senior executives. Strategy constitutes the entrepreneurial function in organizations, and historically this has been the domain of top executives. To a large degree, other managers have been seen as administrators: organizing, directing, and controlling predetermined plans.

More than anything else, however, strategic management is about explaining performance differences among firms and helping managers create economic value. Given this, the central assertion in this book is that much of what separates the performance of firms occurs not at the top but in the middle of organizations, especially in the present business climate. Consider, for example, how shorter product life cycles increase the need for innovation within firms. Global markets are increasingly described as "hypercompetitive" (D'Aveni, 1994), requiring firms to continuously innovate, cannibalizing their own and their competitors' competitive positions. In this confusing and fragmented world, top managers are not in a position to analyze and execute a carefully conceived strategy. The time and information to follow a comprehensive process are not available. Therefore, instead of strategic *decision makers,* top managers are viewed more as strategic *architects*—designers and coordinators of a process, involving people at many levels, that focuses on innovation and leads to the development of new capabilities (Burgelman, 1994; Dutton & Ashford, 1993; Floyd & Wooldridge, 1997).

Stated succinctly, our argument is that rapidly developing technologies and competitive dynamics heighten needs for the renewal of organizational competencies. This puts a premium on new ideas generated at the operating level and creates a shift in the "strategic" responsibilities within organizations. Strategic leadership now occurs not only at the top but at *all* levels of the organization (Nonaka, 1988). Thus, *strategizing* (i.e., the responsibility for thinking and acting strategically) is being radically decentralized (Bartlett & Ghoshal, 1993), and we believe that researchers wanting to study strategic action must adopt a point of view consistent with this reality.

Purpose: A Trojan Horse

When we set out to write this book, our purpose was clear: to elaborate a middle-level perspective on strategy-making processes. As we explored the topic, wrote drafts, and received editorial feedback, however, another goal emerged: to develop a new conceptual framework for strategy process research. Because it was hidden in earlier drafts, Anne Huff described the book's second goal as a "Trojan horse."

Looking back, it became clear that we had identified a set of core constructs and underlying literatures that were different from those in earlier process research. Moreover, whether one adopts a middle-level or some other perspective, it seemed that this new conceptual framework could be useful in developing theory and conducting research. Specifically, rather than focusing on top managers and decision-making processes, our model focuses on divergent ideas, emergent initiatives, and renewed capabilities. To explore these constructs, we were obliged to venture into literatures that generally have not been tapped by process researchers, such as the work on organizational knowledge, social networks, and trust.

At this point, we want to be up-front about reframing the broader discussion and acknowledge that this is both an emergent and a secondary objective of the book. Thinking of the more general process theme as secondary makes sense to us because we think the utility of reconceptualizing process can be demonstrated best by laying out our concern for the role of the middle. We want to make the reader aware that the middle-level approach is by no means the only useful perspective. There are other ways to tap into the newly framed process discussion. For example, it may be fruitful to develop a top management perspective on generating divergent ideas, emergent initiatives, and capability development. Indeed, in smaller companies, we have observed top managers pursuing the development of strategy along much the same lines as we describe here.

The middle-level perspective, however, is most applicable in large, established companies in technologically dynamic, complex, and competitive business environments. In such firms, competitive demands across diverse product and geographic markets create management and control problems of great intricacy. For example, transnational corporations face the need to become globally integrated and locally responsive (Bartlett & Ghoshal, 1993). To address this, a global-geographic matrix has been added to the multidivisional form described by Chandler (1962, 1991).

Matrix structures alone do not solve the problem of formulating strategy, however. In companies such as Asea Brown Boveri (ABB), structure has been redefined from 65 divisions to 1,300 distinct business units. Strategic leadership at the top of the organization has been reduced to the development of vision statements and financial measures (Bartlett & Ghoshal, 1993). The strategy for the business—the entrepreneurial function—has been delegated to those in the middle, that is, the unit managers themselves. Similar realignments have been reported in General Electric Company and elsewhere (Ashkenas, Ulrich, Jick, & Kerr, 1992).

Why a "Middle-Level Perspective"?

We label our focus a "middle-level perspective" for three reasons. First, we want to contrast our approach with the "top management perspective" identified by Hambrick (1988). In the editorial introduction of a special issue of the *Strategic Management Journal*, Hambrick argued that much attention in the field had been devoted to industry and environmental influences and it was time to bring top management back into the picture. Since 1988, many studies have been published that respond to this call. Although useful, this top-level research does not address the problems of strategy formation being described here. We think it is time to focus on the decisions and actions of middle management, to emphasize a "middle-level perspective" in strategic management research.

Second, "middle level" and "middle management" are chosen deliberately over "middle managers." This is not a book about the work of middle managers per se. Rather, it is a book about the strategy-making processes associated with the renewal of organizational capabilities. Our argument is that the information flows and patterns of social influence that transform ideas and initiatives into new capabilities have their nexus at the middle levels of the management hierarchy. Put differently, middle management is "where the action is" in a capability-based view of strategy. But we are not trying to suggest that middle managers have replaced top managers as the "heroes" of the strategic management field. Indeed, the tendency to venerate the decisions of top managers is already too much in evidence (Micklewait & Wooldridge, 1996).

Third, the use of the word *perspective* is also deliberate, and in this context, it has two meanings. First, in a methodological sense, we intend to emphasize a shift in the locus of observation for strategic management research. Literally speaking, we are suggesting that strategy research would profit from observing the behavior of people in the middle. From this vantage point, we believe it is possible to observe the emergence of new social networks and the creation of organizational knowledge that is required in the development of organizational capability. The second meaning of the word *perspective* is Mintzberg's (1983), who contrasts the kind of strategy observed in "bland and lifeless" machine bureaucracies (strategy as a position) with that seen in dynamic organizations (strategy as perspective). "One focuses on the products and markets selected, the other on the business idea conceived, the organization's way of doing things . . . [a process that] requires rich knowledge and mental synthesis" (p. 356). The second view is quite different from the rational analytic view associated with top management decision making. It is much closer, however, to the capability-based view of strategy described here.

In the remainder of this introduction, we outline what we believe to be an emerging view of the strategic renewal process. By "strategic renewal," we mean the process by which organizations develop new capabilities to create or sustain a competitive advantage. In the next section, we explain the intellectual ancestry of strategic renewal and trace three elements of the process: ideas, initiatives, and capabilities. In later chapters, we review bodies of literature relevant to each of these, but at this point, we only want to identify the issues raised by conceptualizing strategy in a way that makes the importance of the middle more explicit.

An Emerging View of the Strategic Renewal Process

Several important theoretical contributions have informed our notion of strategic renewal. As early as 1959, C. E. Lindblom, a political scientist, questioned the idea of "analytically objective" top management decisions formulated to achieve unambiguous goals. Lindblom maintained that policies were developed over time as a consequence of small, seemingly disjointed decisions that were politically acceptable and that moved the organization in small, incremental steps. Although Lindblom stressed the political nature of decision making, his ideas stimulated others, most notably Quinn (1980), to develop the notion of "logical incrementalism." From this viewpoint, strategies are not planned as much as they are emergent. Decisions are made at the last possible moment to take maximum advantage of available information and to minimize strategic risk. Logical incrementalism is perhaps the first conceptualization of strategy as a social learning process. For Quinn, good strategies are not formulated in a comprehensive master plan. Circumstances and assumptions are constantly changing, and it simply is not practical or logical to commit the organization to a major new strategy all at once.

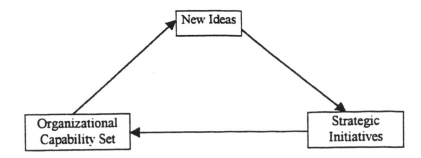

Figure I.1. A General Picture of the Midlevel Strategy Formation Process

Consistent with Quinn, Mintzberg describes strategy as a pattern in a stream of actions and decisions. Again, strategy is more than a discrete decision made at a point in time. Rather, strategy is a living construct that evolves and develops through time. Moreover, Mintzberg's definition points to the presence of multiple actors in the strategy process. Strategy emerges from the activities of participants throughout the organization (Mintzberg & McHugh, 1985).

In sum, Lindblom, Quinn, and Mintzberg are largely responsible for the idea of strategy as something more than a deliberate, rational planning process. They opened up the strategic change process to influence from nonrational, bottom-up organizational forces.

Nonaka (1988) contributes another building block. He describes how strategies emerge through a "middle out" process. Strategies develop from middle-level experiments, expanding outward (laterally) at first, then upward, and, finally, when implemented as part of official strategy, downward. Consistent with this view, Burgelman (1983b, 1988, 1991) depicts autonomous strategies as evolving through an evolutionary process of variation, selection, and retention. Autonomous activities at middle and operating levels generate the requisite variety of strategic alternatives. Then, selection processes force these alternatives to compete with one another for scarce resources. Finally, new strategies are retained when top management ratifies proposals as part of official strategy.

Building on these ideas, Figure I.1 identifies the core elements of a middle-level perspective on strategic renewal. Conceptually, the process begins when an individual within the organization identifies an opportunity or idea that could take the organization in a different strategic direction. Managers choose to pursue some of these divergent ideas and abandon others. Ideas become initiatives when they become associated with a strategic issue and when they begin to receive support within an evolving social network. Initiatives, in turn, evolve into capabilities as members begin to adopt new work routines in the form of feasibility studies, experimental programs, trials, pilot projects, and so on. Finally, surviving ideas are championed by influential actors, and when top management ratifies these, they become part of the organization's capability set.

The three elements shown in the figure may be broadly conceived as a set of process capabilities required for strategic renewal. First, organizations need the ability to generate a variety of divergent ideas (Burgelman, 1983b, 1983c). Importantly, they need access to knowledge that *deviates* from the collective wisdom and that threatens established routines (Floyd & Wooldridge, 1999; Glade, 1967; Nonaka, 1991). We argue that individual subjectivity creates the potential for deviance and that information asymmetries created by weak social ties provide the raw material to fulfill this potential.

Second, strategic renewal requires dynamic and flexible leadership from the middle of the organization. To become strategic initiatives, divergent ideas must be associated with the strategic issues facing the organization. This is part of the interpretation process in organizations, and collective sense making is what transforms individual beliefs into intersubjectively shared beliefs (Weick, 1995). Individuals at middle levels of the organization, in particular, have the knowledge and experience to connect divergent ideas generated from within the organization to strategic issues. In addition, their unique position as a "linking pin" makes them central in the evolution of hierarchical social networks. In the process of sharing an idea, a belief that was once subjective begins to be articulated and thereby becomes more explicit in both its substance and the strategic logic supporting its adoption (Huff & Huff, 2000). This lays the groundwork for broadening the network to include other functional subunits. Moreover, as various middle-level representatives from different subunits interact with one another, they begin to learn new ways of coordinating their behavior. The emergence of trust and the evolution of strong social ties provide the basis for reliable performance. Put differently, these relationships trigger the emergence of new routines and the development of new procedural knowledge in the organization.

Table I.1:   Presumed Connections Between the Top and Middle Level Perspectives
             and Economic Performance

Perspective	Link to Economic Performance
Top Management Perspective	The decisions of top managers to deploy resources and capabilities create advantageous market positions
Middle Management Perspective	Knowledge and social influence processes at the middle level play a key role in determining the organization's ability to innovate and create new capabilities

Finally, the organization needs the ability to integrate new initiatives
and emergent routines into the existing capability set (Burgelman,
1983b, 1983c; Leonard-Barton, 1992; Teece, Pisano, & Shuen, 1997). To
accomplish this, informal support from top management becomes formal sanction, and to preserve coherence, official strategy is redefined to
embrace the new activity (Burgelman, 1991, 1994). What began as informal social interaction becomes established as the routine (Nelson &
Winter, 1982). The potential for conflict is greatest during the ratification phase, however. Top management decree threatens old ways of doing things and undermines the value of old skill sets. Self-interests and
power play a role throughout the process, but at the point of ratification, a new initiative threatens the established order. Thus, the acceptance of new routines and the abandonment of old ones may be determined largely by political processes. In the end, whether there is a level
of commitment sufficient to sustain the initiative and integrate new
routines depends on how members perceive the fairness of the process
and the equity in the resolution.

As portrayed, the process of strategic renewal raises several issues.
Foremost is whether it can be linked to competitive advantage and organizational performance. After all, strategic management is fundamentally distinguished from related fields in organization science by
its focus on organizational performance (Hambrick, 1984). As shown
in Table I.1, the top management perspective is linked to economic performance by virtue of the power that upper echelons wield over how
organizational resources and capabilities are deployed in the market-
place.

Theoretically, the middle-level perspective is linked to organizational performance primarily through the organization's broader, dynamic capability (Nelson, 1991; Teece et al., 1997). Put differently, the knowledge and social influence processes at the middle play a key role in determining the organization's capacity to innovate and renew its capabilities.

Although Table I.1 highlights the positive side of the equation, activities related to both perspectives may also be sources of inertia and thereby link to economic performance in a negative way. When articulated as official goals and strategies, for example, top management decisions limit the attention span of organization members, causing them to focus on particular markets or technologies and to ignore strategically significant change in other domains (Burgelman, 1991, 1994; Huff, Huff, & Thomas, 1992). Similarly, the values and norms that are associated with the development of capabilities and cultivated at middle levels may become a source of "core rigidity" (Leonard-Barton, 1992).

In a recent study (Floyd & Wooldridge, 1997), we examined relationships between middle-level managers' strategic influence behaviors and firm performance. We found strong statistical relationships between middle-level influence and firm performance. Specifically, performance was highest in firms in which middle managers were uniformly involved in downward implementation and *when a subset of managers were engaged in autonomous activities that were likely to take the firm in new strategic directions.*

In one high-performing firm, for example, an idea for a new strategy developed from an experience that an operations manager had while on vacation in Bangkok. For a time, the manager emerged as the driver of a highly visible initiative that expanded the firm's products and distribution channels. Two years later, however, the same manager was spending most of his time involved with everyday details, and he had recently begun helping another manager get started with a new idea. What is key in this example is that the influence of particular managers ebbs and flows over time.

This association between fluid upward influence and organizational performance is consistent with the concept of dynamic capability (Teece et al., 1997). To remain competitive over time, firms develop processes that allow them to accumulate and deploy new capabilities (Porter, 1991). This involves internalizing new ideas from a variety of sources in the operating and competitive environments. The results from our study suggest that middle-level actors are a key part of this process.

However, although there is some evidence that strategic processes at the middle levels (as distinguished from top levels) influence performance, little is known about how the processes depicted in Figure I.1 actually work and how they should be managed. Where, for example, do ideas for new strategies come from? What causes some individuals to see opportunities and strategic options when others do not? In earlier work, we argued that middle management is in a unique position to *synthesize* strategic ideas and advance strategic understanding within organizations (Floyd & Wooldridge, 1992, 1996). Still, many questions concerning the *genesis* of new ideas remain.

Second, how do new ideas coalesce into strategic initiatives? What causes organization members to take risks in the development of an unauthorized project? Again in our earlier work, we identified *facilitating* as a core strategic role in which middle-level management garners informal support and seed resources to develop new initiatives. But how is this done? Why do individuals assume this responsibility, and what determines their success?

Finally, how do middle-level initiatives become part of the organization's capability set? To some extent, this occurs because middle-level actors *champion* strategic proposals to upper management, garnering their official support and sanction. But what else is involved? How do small-scale experimental routines overcome the inertia of existing strategy and structure? How are they transformed into deployable organizational capabilities? And what happens to older, obsolete routines? How are they dismantled and reconfigured?

Overview of the Book

The first step in developing theoretically grounded answers to these questions involves reframing the perspective taken in most strategy research, and that is the fundamental objective of this book. As we have said, the reframing takes two forms—describing renewal from a middle-level perspective and reconceptualizing the theoretical basis for strategy process research. To accomplish these twin goals, we have divided the book into three parts.

Part I: Foundations

In Chapters 1, 2, and 3, we lay out what we see as the foundations for developing a new perspective. Recognizing that many readers may be doctoral students, we take the opportunity in Chapter 1 to provide a short historical account of how the field of strategic management developed, focusing particularly on the origins of the top management perspective as a basis for describing the strategy process. This is important because it provides a sense of the managerial context in which the strategy process literature has evolved and because it shows how deeply rooted the top management perspective has become.

Chapter 2 takes up where Chapter 1 leaves off by reviewing the formal, scientific literature on the strategy process. Even though the chapter is titled "The Top Management Perspective in Strategic Process Research," it also includes the work on emergent strategy. The key point is that studies of emergent strategy depart little from the assumptions used in studies of deliberate strategy.

The last foundational chapter, Chapter 3, answers the "so what" question. Here we distinguish between strategy processes that lead to the accumulation, as opposed to the deployment, of organizational resources. This distinction makes it possible to detail the connections alluded to earlier between the knowledge and social interactions at middle levels of the hierarchy and the renewal of organizational capability. It is at this point, therefore, that we review the recent literature on strategic change and renewal. In many ways, this body of ideas provides the closest connection between organizational processes and capability development. The final step in laying the foundation for our argument, therefore, is justifying a middle-level perspective on strategic renewal. The chapter closes with what we propose as an alternative set of theoretical assumptions for strategy process research.

Part II: New Theoretical Horizons: Organizational Knowledge, Social Networks, and Trust

The second part of the book is devoted to building the theoretical basis for a middle-level perspective. Social relationships and organizational knowledge are the cornerstones of organizational capability, but for the most part, strategy process research has not incorporated the literature relevant to these ideas.

Chapter 4 focuses the discussion on knowledge development. It is knowledge, not information, that is required in the development of new routines and organizational capabilities. Chapter 5 shifts to the analysis of social networks and organizational trust to show how knowledge is absorbed and disseminated within organizations. In many ways, social network analysis provides a window into the evolutionary aspects of strategy. In particular, we think this literature suggests an explanation for the migration of divergent ideas and initiatives across external and internal organizational boundaries.

In reviewing this literature, we are providing the reader with a summary of the ideas we encountered as we wrote the book. In that sense, these chapters reflect the intellectual ingredients of the middle-level model that we develop in the third part of the book. In another sense, however, we are pointing to ideas that we think are becoming increasingly central to strategy process research from whatever perspective the researcher chooses to take. We hope readers who are interested in the broader agenda will find these reviews helpful at least as a starting point for their research. Readers who are more interested in what we mean by a middle-level perspective and who are already versed in the relevant literatures may want to skip directly to Part III.

Part III: A Middle-Level Perspective

In the third part of the book, we move from synthesizing existing research toward the development of a model for conducting research from a middle-level perspective. Chapter 6 elaborates the idea-initiative-capability cycle on the basis of the literature on social networks, organizational knowledge, and trust. This generates a series of descriptive propositions that catalog critical "touch points" of strategic renewal. More than a catalog of issues, however, Chapter 6 is our attempt to describe a substantive theory. By this point in the book, we hope to have provoked readers to develop their own questions and possible answers. The last chapter more formally describes research and methodological issues raised by a middle-level perspective. We appraise several pieces of research that we consider exemplars of a middle-level approach, and we outline the empirical procedures we feel are most likely to yield further insight into the role of middle-level actors.

In discussing this book with colleagues, we are frequently challenged on the notion that top managers take a backseat to other organization

members in strategic renewal. We are not the first to make such arguments, but still, the sharpness of the barbs thrown our way has been
surprising. Partly, this may be because of philosophical differences,
such as what we mean by "strategy" and how "strategy" differs from
"operations." Partly, it may be because of vested interests in research
streams built within the top management perspective. Whatever its
cause, we have no objection to intellectual skepticism. We ask only that
readers try to use this book as a way to develop a healthy sense of doubt
about their *own* preconceptions, because it is from such doubt that
lively debates emerge. Though we do not consider the middle-level perspective a new scientific paradigm, we think the spirit of Kuhn's (1962)
analysis applies.

> If a [new perspective] is ever to triumph it must gain some first supporters,
> men [sic] who will develop it to the point where hardheaded arguments can
> be produced and multiplied. And even those arguments, when they come,
> are not individually decisive. Because scientists are reasonable men, one or
> another argument will ultimately persuade many of them. But there is no
> single argument that can or should persuade them all. (p. 158)

I
Foundations

1 Foundations of the Strategic Management Field

At its origins, strategic management was imprinted with the notion that strategy research is about helping top managers determine appropriate strategy and install necessary implementation mechanisms. . . . Although there were already voices for alternative arguments (e.g., Bower, 1970), the vast majority of published research in the newly emerging field focused on strategy content and the problems of top management.

As an applied area of study, the field of strategic management has its roots in practice. Indeed, many of the seminal works in the field, such as Igor Ansoff's (1965) *Corporate Strategy* and Alfred Sloan's (1972) *My Years With General Motors,* were contributed not by academics but by practicing managers wishing to reflect on and expand what they had learned during long tenures as corporate executives. Thus, in contrast to disciplines marked by long theoretical or methodological traditions, strategy as a field of inquiry developed from a practical need to better understand the reasons for success and failure among organizations (Rumelt, Schendel, & Teece, 1994). This focus on overall organizational performance and the influence of early contributors naturally oriented the field toward senior management.

Many reviewers trace the academic discipline of strategy to the early 1960s and three defining works: Chandler's (1962) *Strategy and Structure,* Ansoff's (1965) *Corporate Strategy,* and Andrews's (1971) *The Concept of Corporate Strategy* (Rumelt et al., 1994). Extrapolations from practice, these works reflected the economic and managerial arrangements of their time, including hierarchical power and functional specialization. Principles of scientific management (Taylor, 1947) dominated the design of large organizations. Work was divided into small components, and managers were encouraged to optimize subunit efficiencies, leaving company-wide issues to top management.

The assumptions about strategy implicit in such early discourse had an "imprinting" effect on the institution of strategic management (DiMaggio, 1988; Scott, 1995). The approach of early authors was incorporated into subsequent research; as a result, they imparted certain core assumptions about how strategy is made and who is involved in making it.

One could add other writers, such as Chester Barnard (1938), Russell Ackoff (1970), and Herbert Simon (1957), in describing the headwaters of the strategy field. They too were influential in creating and imprinting what we are calling "the top management perspective." But Chandler, Ansoff, and Andrews were especially fundamental in creating the prevailing view that strategy is made at the top and executed at the bottom.

Chandler's *Strategy and Structure*

No book has had a greater impact on the development of strategic management as an academic discipline than Alfred Chandler's (1962) *Strategy and Structure: Chapters in the History of the American Industrial Enterprise.* Chandler, a business historian at Harvard, set out to tell the story of the growth of large businesses during the first half of the 20th century. He did so through detailed case experiences of four firms: Dupont, Sears, General Motors, and Standard Oil of New Jersey.[1] Each of these firms experienced rapid growth during the early part of the century, and consistent with the thinking of the day, Chandler expected to relate a story of how growth per se had required these firms to adopt new organizational forms. He found instead that, rather than size itself, increased complexity, from expanded geographic and product/market scope (i.e., a change in strategy), accounted for changes in organizational structure.

The book is best known, therefore, for its conclusion that organizational structures must be adapted to changes in strategy; that is, *struc-*

ture follows strategy. Fundamentally, this conclusion suggests a sequential process in which strategy is centrally determined first and then implemented through an appropriate organizational structure. Chandler, however, tempers this conclusion in the introduction to the 1989 edition of the book: "Thus structure had as much impact on strategy as strategy had on structure. . . . My goal from the start was to study the complex interconnections in a modern industrial enterprise between structure and strategy, and an ever-changing external environment" (1962/1989, intro. p. 3).

The recognition that structure is not only determined by strategy but also affects it is critical to a sophisticated understanding of the strategy process reflected in Chandler's case data (Burgelman, 1983c). Nonetheless, the prominence of the structure-follows-strategy thesis had an important impact on the development of strategic management theory, and it has done much to focus the field's attention exclusively on top management. Indeed, following Chandler, both Ansoff and Andrews adopt the structure-follows-strategy assumption in their work, using it to create a distinction between management's strategic and tactical responsibilities.

Chandler (1962) observed that the structures created in response to new strategies included four managerial levels: field units, departmental headquarters, the central office, and the general office. Each level dealt with problems of different time frames and scope. "At the top is a *general office.* There, general executives and staff specialists coordinate, appraise, and plan goals and policies and allocate resources" (p. 9). In this discussion, strategy appears to occur at the general office level, and it is executives at this level who are largely credited for the success or failure of the organization.

> Although the enterprise undoubtedly had a life of its own above and beyond that of its individual executives, . . . its health and effectiveness in carrying out its basic economic functions depended almost entirely on the talents of its [top] administrators. (Chandler, 1962, p. 384)

Ansoff's *Corporate Strategy*

Whereas *Strategy and Structure* is a historical treatise chronicling the growth of large enterprise in the American economy, Igor Ansoff's

Corporate Strategy (1965) was written for "working managers" to provide "a practical method for strategic decision making." Ansoff explicitly addressed the book to the executives he saw as responsible for making strategic decisions: "the chairman of the board, board members, the president, the chief financial officer, and planning staffs which report to them" (p. ix). Thus, from the outset, it is clear that Ansoff saw strategy making as a centralized activity. This becomes more evident as the book unfolds.

The book provides an important foundation for the strategy field in that it introduces and defines constructs (e.g., synergy, competitive advantage, competence, and capability) that have remained central within the discipline. Importantly, Ansoff also introduces the idea that strategy means creating a "match" between the organization and its environment. Developing this notion, he observes that strategic decisions are made under conditions of uncertainty, in partial ignorance, and that they are nonrepetitive, and not self-regenerative. Thus, if executives do not proactively address strategic issues, their lives will be dominated by operating concerns.

To make strategic issues explicit and to aid executives in making strategic choices, Ansoff develops a "system of objectives." At the highest level is the firm's long-term maximization of rate of return. This is then translated into a series of shorter-term "proximate objectives," both economic and noneconomic. As a guide to strategy, the system constitutes a "rule for making decisions." Given partial ignorance and uncertainty in the environment, however, "last minute executive judgment is required," and thus, from Ansoff's viewpoint, strategic decisions cannot be "delegated downward" (Ansoff, 1965, p. 119).

Harvard: *The Concept of Corporate Strategy*

Attributed to Kenneth Andrews, the first theoretical material to accompany cases appeared in the Harvard textbook *Business Policy: Text and Cases* (Learned, Christensen, Andrews, & Guth, 1965). The text begins by defining business policy as "the study of the functions and responsibilities of senior management" (p. 3). It is divided into two parts: *Book One: Determining Corporate Strategy* and *Book Two: Implementing Corporate Strategy.* The distinction mirrors Chandler's, once again presuming a sequential process in which a centrally developed strategy is deliberately implemented. Even today, the formulation-implementation framework remains the dominant scheme used to classify chapters in most contemporary strategy textbooks.

Much of the Andrews text introduces policy students to concepts developed elsewhere (e.g., Selznick's, 1957, distinctive competence and Tilles's, 1963, criteria for evaluating corporate strategy), but its most original contribution is SWOT analysis. This framework prescribes a match between external opportunities and threats and internal strengths and weaknesses so that senior executives can be "analytically objective" in their formulation of strategy.

Table 1.1 summarizes how Chandler, Ansoff, and Andrews helped establish the top management perspective within the strategy field. This is not a criticism of the authors' work. Indeed, it appears that the top management perspective became established more as a by-product of these authors' efforts than through their intent. Chandler's concern, for example, was to establish a historical record for the emergence of new organizational forms during a unique period in the country's economic development. He did not set out to create a new field of inquiry, nor is it likely that he anticipated how narrowly and literally the structure-follows-strategy thesis would be interpreted. For their part, Ansoff, as a senior executive for the Rand Corporation, and Andrews, as a faculty member and consultant, had experienced the frustrations of grappling with strategic problems in an era devoid of theory. Their motivations had less to do with process than with providing decision makers with tools for reducing the inherent complexity underlying strategic issues.

The 1970s and the Emergence of "Corporate Planning"

The early contributors to strategy assumed away organizational process issues. The activities taking place in the middle of organizations were seen largely as "administrative," secondary to top-level strategic decision making. By the late 1960s, however, most large corporations had established "long-range" planning and budgeting systems, and the management of these systems increasingly became a dominant issue.

A representative planning system required managers at various levels to fill out detailed forms concerning revenues (sales projections), operating expenses, and capital expenditures. From these inputs, divi-

Table 1.1   The Genesis of the Top Management Perspective

Author	Contribution	Implication
Chandler	Structure follows strategy	Sequential view of strategy making
	Distinguishing strategic from tactical administrative tasks	Identification of strategic tasks with top levels of organizational hierarchy
	Allocation of resources key to organizational success	Credits top managers with success of organization
Ansoff	Practical system for making strategic decisions	Frames strategic process as problem of top management decision making
	Match between organization and its environment	Uncertainty and imperfect information require that strategic decisions be made at the top
Andrews	Separates formulation from implementation	Solidifies strategy process sequence
	SWOT analysis	Presents formulation as "analytically objective"

sional controllers and staff planners compiled "5-year plans," typically including income statements broken down by product line, pro forma balance sheets for 5 years, and the next year's operating budgets. Unfortunately, in many cases, the planning exercise came to be seen as a "waste of time." As one manager put it, "Once the plan had been approved, we filed it away in a drawer and forgot about it. Operating decisions and capital budgeting decisions were made as if the plan didn't exist" (Abell & Hammond, 1979, p. 4).

In response to growing frustrations with planning systems, the 1970s gave rise to a variety of efforts designed to advance the practice of planning within large corporations. Writers of this period wrote books and articles describing what they believed to be exemplary corporate planning and advancing their own notions of best practice (e.g., Gilbert & Lorange, 1974; Steiner, 1970; Vancil, 1976). Although prescientific, these writings represent the field's first "process" literature and provide the early hints that strategy occurs (or should occur) at multiple levels in organizations. According to these formal planners, not only do executives at the highest organizational echelons plan, but managers of subunits also create objectives and programs for their areas as well.

Thus, planning systems should be developed as mechanisms to coordinate and achieve consistency among various plans and activities occurring throughout the organization (Vancil & Lorange, 1975). Such systems should be iterative, and since decisions at higher levels place constraints on lower levels, a certain amount of negotiation should be expected as corporate-wide objectives get translated into operating activities.

A key insight of this literature was that plans produced by staff planners were ineffective and that line managers needed to be involved in the process. Although attention was given to involving line managers (Gilbert & Lorange, 1974), their participation was explicitly limited by their position in the hierarchy. Managers at middle and lower levels supported the development of centralized plans by providing information upward and receiving direction from above. For the most part, managers' substantive planning responsibilities took place from their level down (Vancil, 1976). Thus, the planning literature of the 1970s presents a distinctly deliberate form of strategy in which top management articulates long-term (e.g., 5-year) objectives that are then translated into subactivities, operating budgets, and action plans. The role of middle- and lower-level managers is limited to "planning implementation"—that is, how areas under their authority address the priorities of those above them.

PIMS, the BCG, and the Search for the "Laws of the Market"

During this period, while many were focusing on ways to improve planning processes, others focused attention on the development of "market laws" and analytic tools that would allow firms to plan more "strategically." The PIMS (Profit Impact of Market Strategies) project was established at the General Electric (GE) Company in 1960 to better understand the performance of its operating divisions. After several years of data collection, GE developed a regression model that "explained" a significant part of the variance in divisional return on investment.

Over time, the project expanded beyond GE, moving first to the Harvard Business School and eventually to the Marketing Science Institute. By the end of the 1970s, more than 1,200 business units from more than

200 Fortune 500 companies were represented in the PIMS database, and PIMS researchers had published an impressive set of findings in a series of highly influential *Harvard Business Review* articles (Buzzell, Gale, & Sultan, 1975; Schoefler, Buzzell, & Heany, 1974). The findings from these early studies pointed to the importance of two factors—industry attractiveness and relative competitive position.

Independently of the PIMS project, the Boston Consulting Group (BCG) had been gathering evidence and advancing interest in what came to be known as the "experience curve." According to this concept, costs decline predictably as cumulative output increases. Market share leaders, therefore, who presumably have the most experience, also have the lowest cost. The experience curve provided a logical explanation for the PIMS findings.

The discovery of such regularities began to shift the priorities of many firms. At the business level, the objective was to "buy" market share, often at any cost. At the corporate level, top managers began to think in portfolio terms. Frameworks such as the GE growth-share matrix and the BCG grid appeared on the scene. The era of strategy had truly arrived. Unfortunately, in too many cases, strategy was oversimplified to selling the kennel, milking the cows, and feeding the children.

Aside from the simplistic applications that often accompanied them, the arrival of analytical tools, backed by "scientific evidence," perpetuated the notion of strategy as an exclusively top management, "analytically objective" function. Armed with statistical evidence, underlying theory, and expensively paid consultants, top managers were now on firm ground, able to orchestrate the success of their corporations from above. At the corporate level, portfolio techniques could be used to arrive at rational investment and divestment decisions. At the business level, unequivocal priorities could be set in market share terms.

Strategic Management:
A New View of Business Policy and Planning

As the 1970s drew to a close, academics interested in strategic issues were increasingly frustrated by the field's lack of scholarly credibility. The limitations of formal planning had become apparent during the turbulent economy of the '70s, and its prominence as a topic of interest had gradually declined. Besides, the planning literature was largely normative and decidedly practitioner-oriented—not at all the tone of university research. Perhaps more telling, the important conceptual breakthroughs of the era (e.g., BCG's growth-share matrix and the PIMS studies) had been developed by consulting houses rather than by scholars. To compound the problem, there were no academic publications devoted to strategic management research. Because the field was ill defined and lacking any accepted conceptual framework, few journals would seriously consider strategic management research.

In 1977, a group of scholars from around the United States participated in a conference organized to address these concerns. Following the conference, the organizers, Professor Dan E. Schendel of Purdue University and Charles W. Hofer, then at Columbia, created an edited volume of papers and commentaries solicited from those who were beginning to speak for an emerging perspective. To commission the papers and organize them into the volume, Schendel and Hofer developed what they referred to as a new paradigm for business policy—strategic management.

Table 1.2 reproduces the elements of the Schendel and Hofer (1979) paradigm. The framework is significant for its delineation of the components underlying strategy and for its description of issues that are relevant at the various strategy levels. But from our perspective, the framework's most significant characteristic is its elaboration of a sequential strategy process. The authors note that the formulation-implementation sequence is not always as depicted: Evaluation and implementation may precede formulation. Still, the two tasks of strategic management are presented as discrete and, for the most part, separable in both theory and practice.

This conceptual elaboration of strategic management into subactivities demonstrated strategy's importance within organizations. Now, "no manager . . . except those at the very lowest operating level [was] without some responsibilities in the strategic management process" (Schendel & Hofer, 1979, p. 14). As important, the subactivities defined clear roles for managers at various levels, essentially driven from the top down. Mid- and lower-level managers, for example, might be expected to inform top managers of events occurring in the external environment, but they were unlikely to participate in the formulation of strategies for coping with these events.

The separation of formulation from implementation is consistent with earlier conceptualizations. "Implementation is different from the previous tasks" of goal formulation, environmental analysis, strategy formulation, and strategy evaluation because it "is inherently behav-

Table 1.2   Central Elements of the Schendel and Hofer (1979) Paradigm

---

- Strategic management is a process that deals with the entrepreneurial work of the organization, with organizational renewal and growth, and, more particularly, with developing and utilizing the strategy that is to guide the organization's operations.
- The concept of strategy is built around four components:
  1. scope
  2. resource deployments/distinctive competencies
  3. competitive advantage
  4. synergy
- Strategy occurs at three organizational levels:
  1. Corporate: What business should we be in?
  2. Business: How should the firm compete in a given business?
  3. Functional: The integration of subfunctional activities and the integration of functional areas with the environment.
- Other elements include the following:
  Organizational goal formulation
  Environmental analysis
  Strategy formulation
  Strategy evaluation
  Strategy implementation
  Strategic control

---

ioral in nature," as opposed to rational and analytical (Schendel & Hofer, 1979, p. 17). In our view, separating formulation from implementation in this way artificially separates the "thinking" element of strategy from its "doing" element. This creates the notion that top managers are "thinkers," who formulate strategy, while other organizational members are "doers," responsible for its execution.

More subtly, the separation advances the notion that only top managers can be expected to act as responsible custodians of the organization's interests. Implementation is said to involve the design of six elements that "impact behaviors" in the organization: (a) standards, (b) measures, (c) incentives, (d) rewards, (e) penalties, and (f) controls (Christensen, Andrews, Bower, Hamermesh, & Porter, 1982, p. 636). In other words, not only does the separation focus the field's attention on top-level decision making, but it also makes assumptions about the nature of others working within organizations. First, it suggests that they cannot be expected to think about issues of strategy. Their job is merely to "do" (Mintzberg, 1990). Second, the emphasis on controlling behavior suggests that most organizational actors are motivated by opportunism and narrow self-interest. In light of this, it is not surprising that middle-level management has not been seen as a substantive contributor to strategy. Indeed, it has often been seen as an obstacle (Guth & MacMillan, 1986).

The Schendel and Hofer (1979) volume represents an important milestone in the development of the strategic management field. The framework it provided served to organize disparate threads of literature and identified the field's research needs. Despite the concerns just noted, this work seemed poised to move beyond the artificial formulation-implementation dichotomy and ready to tackle the more complex issues of strategy *formation*. The authors observed,

> Strategy formulation . . . has received more attention than any of the other tasks in the strategic management process. . . . The reconciliation of social/political processes used in implementation with analytical/rational processes used in strategy formulation and evaluation represents another major research challenge for the strategic management area. (pp. 16-17)

Competitive Strategy:
Techniques for Analyzing Industries and Competitors

In 1980, however, Michael Porter published the highly influential book *Competitive Strategy*. Aside from Chandler's work, no other book has had a more profound impact on how the strategy field has progressed. In essence, this book translates concepts from industrial organization economics and applies them to the problem of strategy formulation. In so doing, it provides a theoretical richness to strategic management, greatly enhancing the analysis of the external opportunities and threats contained in Andrews's (1971) model. In addition, the book was among the first to introduce a classification scheme of substantive competitive strategies. Like the Miles and Snow (1978) typology that immediately preceded it, Porter's "generic" strategies provide the field with a parsimonious way to characterize and consider a firm's competitive positions.

The profound appeal of *Competitive Strategy* is easy to understand. For practitioners, it provided a set of tangible and readily assessable factors that could greatly amplify understanding of the firm's competitive situation. For researchers, the well-developed constructs and underlying theory from economics were a seductive force in a field struggling to achieve academic status. Suddenly, the field possessed important theory, operational constructs, and proven methodologies.

The 1980s were marked by the growth of "scientific" research investigating relationships implied by economic theory. Representative research of this era examined relationships between various market conditions and the efficacy of alternative strategic approaches. Underlying this research was the now well-established assumption that strategies could be formulated, "independently of the organization" (Schendel & Hofer, 1979, p. 17), through analytical, objective processes. Although this strategy content research made many important contributions, greatly increasing the field's understanding of how various competitive forces interrelate, in one respect it was a diversion—drawing researchers away from a sophisticated treatment of process issues.

Conclusion

At its origins, strategic management was imprinted with the notion that strategy research is about helping top managers determine appropriate strategy and install necessary implementation mechanisms. Some of this imprinting was in the form of direct descriptions of the planning process and some of it was indirect—focusing attention on the analytical techniques top managers needed to create, evaluate, and control strategy. Although there were already voices for alternative arguments (e.g., Bower, 1970), the vast majority of published research in the newly emerging field focused on strategy content and the problems of top management.

In the next chapter, we suggest that this orientation—and the core assumptions attendant to it—continued to haunt strategy research even after it took a decided turn toward process. The "top management perspective" is the genesis for virtually every hypothesis in empirical work, and most theoretical work has moved under the same assumptions. Perhaps because of this focus, the field has made considerable progress. By the end of Chapter 2, however, we will suggest that it is time to stretch old assumptions and consider an alternative, middle-level view.

Note

1. The case data were then augmented with confirming evidence from nearly 100 of the era's largest industrial firms.

2 The Top Management Perspective in Strategic Process Research

This view contends that performance of an organization is ultimately a reflection of its top managers. (Hambrick, 1987, p. 88)

The last chapter described how the strategic management field evolved to adopt a "top management perspective." In this chapter, we continue our review of the field, examining strategy process research done since 1980. Our purpose is to demonstrate how the focus on top management has limited researchers' conception of the strategy process. In particular, the review highlights research characterizing strategy making as being predominantly a decision-making process. By drawing attention to this often-implicit assumption, the chapter lays the groundwork for the remainder of the book, which argues that strategy formation is a middle-level social learning process.

Strategy Making as a Decision Process

As stated above, the notion of strategy as centered in top management has often resulted in the strategy process being characterized as decision making. Typically, a distinction has been made between the "analytically objective" formulation process and the political/behavioral implementation process (Andrews, 1971; Chappell & Huff, 1998; Fredrickson, 1984; Pettigrew, 1992).

Eisenhardt and Zbaracki (1992) divide the strategic decision making literature into three subgroups: bounded rationality, politics and power, and "garbage can" models. This division is appealing because, in the broadest terms, each of these streams represents a "model" of how strategic decisions come about. Furthermore, the categories play off one another's weaknesses, and as a group, they appear to offer a broad and robust explanation of strategic decision making.

The rational approach was improved by arguments for bounded rationality (Cyert & March, 1963; Simon, 1957). This is a reaction to classical economics that presumes strategy as resulting from the decisions of imperfectly informed, goal-satisficing actors. Beginning in the early 1980s, proponents also moved toward adopting a contingency framework. Here, the degree of rationality is argued to range along a continuum from purely synoptic to purely incremental, depending mainly on the level of uncertainty and change in the environment. Moreover, the process in most organizations is said to be composed of "mixed modes" (Fredrickson, 1984; Fredrickson & Mitchell, 1984; Mintzberg, 1978).

The political model begins by asserting that organizations consist of coalitions or groups of people with conflicting interests (Allison, 1971; Pettigrew, 1973; Quinn, 1980). Strategic decisions follow from the desires and choices of the most powerful group or "dominant coalition" (Hinings, Hickson, Pennings, & Schneck, 1974; March, 1962; Salancik & Pfeffer, 1974). Rational decision processes, such as goal setting and planning, play a role in the political model, but such activities are subsumed within a broader, "more realistic" framework (Quinn, 1980). Theorists in the political camp continue to debate whether conflict among competing interests is collectively rational (Quinn, 1980) or simply a distasteful waste of resources (Dean & Sharfman, 1992; Eisenhardt & Bourgeois, 1988).

Ostensibly, the "garbage can" model denies the rationality of strategic decisions outright. Inconsistent priorities, unclear technologies, and mercurial participation surround decisions with so much ambiguity that strategy occurs only as a haphazard confluence of people, problems, solutions, and opportunities (Cohen, March, & Olsen, 1972). In this view, strategic decision making is not rational and organized as much as it is chaotic.

Without concerning ourselves here about the validity of any of these positions, it is interesting to observe what they have in common. The common thread running throughout decision-making research is its grounding in the concept of rationality. Taking cognitive limitations into account, for example, Fredrickson (1984) asserts that the utility of comprehensiveness (i.e., rationality) in strategy depends on the stability of the environment. Quinn (1980), on the other hand, argues that incrementalism is more "logical" (i.e., more rational) when one considers the internal political realities along with the external uncertainties that surround the decision process. Even "organized anarchy" makes sense as a concept only when it is compared against the rational baseline; to understand what chaos means, one needs a sense of order.

To be rational, in the most minimalist sense, decisions must reflect an ordering of human preferences. In the purely rational model, such ordering is achieved by analyzing alternative means (or strategies) according to the extent to which they lead to a clearly defined end (or goal). In a boundedly rational model, the preferred option is selected based on its ability to satisfy criteria at least as well as other known alternatives. In the political model, conflicts over alternative solutions are settled by the preferences of the most powerful coalition. Even in the garbage can model, empirical studies suggest that the conditions under which there is *no* preference ranking are extremely rare. Ultimately, some kind of criterion emerges, though often in a more or less random fashion (Levitt & Nass, 1989; Magjuka, 1988). In fact, Eisenhardt and Zbaracki (1992) remark that even the garbage can model "may more accurately be described as an extreme form of bounded rationality" (p. 31).

The pervasiveness of rationality in the strategic decision-making literature and the consequent reliance on preference ordering reveal the first of three fundamental assumptions we observe in the strategy process literature: Strategic decisions result from a process of ranking alternatives according to decision criteria. Put differently, questions within the organization about which strategy to pursue are settled by referring to a higher-order principle, often expressed as a desired end state or goal.

Although derived as a principle of rationality, the appeal to goals is wedded closely to organization theory's focus on goal conflict among individual members as a barrier to coherent action (Lawrence & Lorsch, 1967; March & Simon, 1958). Theories of bureaucratic authority relationships (Weber, 1947) and organizational control (Ouichi, 1980) have developed as mechanisms to institutionalize hierarchical preference criteria and thereby coordinate behavior. Thus, a core assumption of the field can be found at the intersection of organization and decision theory. In addition, this part of the field's intellectual ancestry further explains why so much attention centers on the upper reaches of the organizational hierarchy.

Research on Top Management Teams

Operating under the assumption that top management's decision behavior explains why "organizations act as they do" (Hambrick & Mason, 1984), a great deal of research since 1980 has been concerned with the conduct of top management teams (TMTs). This body of work can be divided into two streams: one that investigates actual decision processes within the TMT and another that focuses on the characteristics of the TMT itself.

TMT Decision Processes

Characteristic of TMT decision process research are studies that investigate the comprehensiveness of decision processes (Fredrickson, 1984); consensual versus conflict-based decision processes (Schweiger, Sandberg, & Rechner, 1989); TMT agreement on goals and means (Dess & Origer, 1987); cognitive processes (Barr, Stimpert, & Huff, 1992); and the speed with which top managers make strategic decisions (Eisenhardt & Bourgeois, 1988). Although the number of field studies is growing (Eisenhardt, 1989; Eisenhardt & Bourgeois, 1988; Johnson, 1988; Miller, Kets de Vries, & Toulouse, 1982; Reger & Huff, 1993), many studies have used laboratory designs (Schweiger, Sandberg, & Ragan, 1986; Schweiger et al., 1989; Schwenk, 1984), questionnaires (Dess, 1987), or archival data (Barr et al., 1992).

TMT Characteristics

Work in this area has focused on the psychological makeup of top managers and the composition of top management teams. In the first case, it is theoretically transparent that a manager's psychology will af-

The Situation (Environmental and Organizational Information)	TMT Characteristics (e.g. Heterogeneity, Tenure, Education) and Thought Processes (e.g. Consensus, Conflict, Mental Models)	Organizational Outcomes (Organizational Strategy and Performance)

Figure 2.1. Presumed Causal Links in Research on the Top Management Team
SOURCE: Adapted from Hambrick and Mason (1984).

fect his or her decisions. Theory, then, has elaborated connections between various psychological predispositions and strategic choices. Because "top executives probably are quite reluctant to participate" in studies that use psychological measures (Hambrick & Mason, 1984, p. 196), most studies have relied on surrogate measures (e.g., tenure in the organization, level of education, functional background, etc.) to explain the content of senior management's strategic decisions. Using similar measures, work on the composition of top management teams has developed theory and conducted research into the effect of TMT homogeneity and heterogeneity on strategic outcomes under various conditions. Hurst, Rush, and White (1989), for example, argue for the importance of team heterogeneity in contexts requiring strategic renewal. Wiersema and Bantel (1993) use path analysis to study the effect of environment and TMT heterogeneity on TMT turnover.

Despite the diversity of content and richness of method in this research, it is based on a relatively simple model of the strategy process. As shown in Figure 2.1, the social and psychological processes within the TMT are viewed as causes of the strategic choices they make, and these choices are seen to be related directly to organizational strategy and performance.

It would be wrong to suggest that scholars in this domain subscribe to the simple model in Figure 2.1 as a complete picture of strategy making. Still, this is the conceptual framework guiding their selection of variables and research design. In addition to hierarchical ordering, two additional assumptions of strategy process research seem clear. First, researchers overwhelmingly assume that information from the environment and the organization is encountered predominantly by top managers, who thoughtfully process it and knowledgeably formulate strategy. Second, once a strategic choice has been made, research has assumed that the decision is directly linked to organizational action and performance.

The assumption that strategy results from top management thinking about the organization and its fit with the environment appears inevitable in this research. In a conceptual paper, for example, Priem (1990) argues that associations between top management heterogeneity and firm performance are governed by how much variation exists in the firm's environment. More consensus, and hence more homogeneity, is desirable in stable environments, and the opposite is true under dynamic conditions. Similarly, the conceptual framework for Wiersema and Bantel's (1993) study is that "top executives must be vigilant in their monitoring of environmental conditions to determine whether the current fit with the firm is appropriate" (p. 485). Cognitive researchers are equally explicit: "Organizational renewal requires that a firm's top managers make timely adjustments in their mental models following significant changes in the environment" (Barr et al., 1992, p. 15). In short, throughout this research, there is presumed to be a direct link between environmental information and top management thought processes.

The presumed link between TMT thinking and the execution of realized strategy is equally evident. Indeed, in calling for research on the upper echelon, Hambrick and Mason (1984) assumed that "organizational outcomes—both strategies and effectiveness—are viewed as reflections of the values and cognitive bases" (p. 193) of top managers. More dramatically, "This view contends that performance of an organization is ultimately a reflection of its top managers" (Hambrick, 1987, p. 88). The direct connection between thinking, strategic decisions, and organizational performance is also explicit in research on consensus and conflict within the TMT (Dess, 1987; Dess & Origer, 1987; Schweiger et al., 1986; Schweiger et al., 1989; Wooldridge & Floyd, 1989).

Table 2.1 summarizes three major premises in research on strategic decision making and top management teams and, for illustration purposes, connects these assumptions with propositions emanating from specific studies. Many readers will find the assumptions unproblematic and perhaps self-evident, and, as noted, the researchers doing this research would likely admit that the assumptions represent "necessary simplifications." Indeed, our purpose is not to refute the utility of these assumptions, for they have been useful in generating a substantial body of knowledge. Rather, our objective is to deepen the reader's appreciation for how deeply these assumptions are ingrained in the strategy process tradition.

Evolving Toward a Broader Perspective

We now turn to research that recognizes the role of actors beyond top management. Here, again, we will argue that even this work has been shaped by the assumptions listed in Table 2.1. Still, the contributions described here represent a springboard enabling the development of a midlevel perspective. In particular, we pay attention to three contributions (Burgelman, 1983b; Hart, 1992; Mintzberg & Waters, 1985) that we view as important in the evolution of a new perspective on strategy process research. As we proceed, we highlight the key insights that each of these suggests for the midlevel perspective we are developing.

A number of writers in the management literature made early contributions to a general understanding of the middle management challenge (Keys & Bell, 1982; Uyterhoven, 1972) but were not focused on understanding their strategic role. Rosabeth Moss Kanter's (1982, 1983) work on middle management and innovation and the cases in Bower (1970) provide excellent sources of clinical data. These did not provide the theoretical foundation needed for further research, however. Leonard Sayles's work on leadership (1993) is foundational in the sense that it stimulated both Burgelman and Mintzberg, but, again, Sayles is focused on middle management in a broader sense, including operational as well as strategic activities. Finally, Stuart Hart's (1992) paper provided a unique integration of theory from the "traditional" process school and concepts in emergent strategy. This helped us (and surely many others) put the pieces of a disparate field together.

This review will not address research on the management of strategy implementation. Implementation is an important part of the strategic process, and the ideas and findings of research on the topic (in particular, Galbraith & Kazanjian, 1986; Hrebiniak & Joyce, 1984; Nutt, 1987) are an important part of the context for defining middle management's substantive role. In this chapter, however, we are concerned with research that approaches strategy as a bottom-up process that thereby allows for a "formulation" effect from middle management. In fact, we

Table 2.1   Critical Assumptions in the Strategy Process Literature That Obscure
the Importance of the Middle

1. Strategic choice results from a process of hierarchical ordering.
   - Depending on the degree of environmental stability, strategic alternatives are selected through a comprehensive process (Fredrickson & Mitchel, 1984).
   - Political conflicts over strategic options are settled by the dominant individual or coalition (Quinn, 1980).
   - Strategies are made as a result of the random emergence of pseudorational decision criteria (Cohen, March, & Olsen, 1972).
2. Information from the environment and organization is encountered by top management, who process it and formulate the organization's strategy.
   - Environmental complexity is positively associated with demographic heterogeneity within the TMT (Wiersema & Bantel, 1993).
   - TMT consensus is associated with organizational performance in competitive environments (Dess, 1987).
   - High cognitive complexity is required from top managers to cope with the environmental complexity of multidivisional firms (Calori, Johnson, & Sarnin, 1994).
3. Once the choice has been made, top management decisions lead directly to organizational outcomes.
   - Greater levels of TMT heterogeneity are associated with higher levels of corporate diversification (Michel & Hambrick, 1992).
   - Interpersonal conflict is associated with higher-quality strategic decisions among top management groups (Schweiger & Sandberg, 1989).
   - There is a curvilinear relationship between TMT homogeneity/heterogeneity and firm performance (Priem, 1990).

consider the distinction between formulation and implementation in the strategy process a pedagogical convenience but a theoretical hurdle to understanding the full range of influence that various actors have on the formation of realized strategy. Thus, implementation research cannot provide the springboard for a midlevel perspective because it is firmly rooted in the idea that top management creates strategy while middle management "installs" it (Nutt, 1987).

From Strategic Decisions to Strategy Making

Few people have had as much influence on the field of strategic management, and on strategy process research in particular, as Henry Mintzberg. In 1985, he and James Waters published "Of Strategies, Deliberate and Emergent," which reflected the findings of several research studies conducted over a period of years (Mintzberg, 1972, 1978;

Mintzberg & Waters, 1982, 1984). It could be argued that Mintzberg's work created a paradigm shift in the way we think about strategy, and for that reason, we take up his theory of emergent strategy first.

The core concept in Mintzberg's theory is the definition of *strategy* itself: "Strategy [is] a 'pattern in a stream of decisions' " (Mintzberg & Waters, 1985, p. 257). Defining strategy in this way means that "strategic" actions occur in many different parts of the organization. Strategies are historical patterns in organizational behavior that can be "isolated . . . and identified as . . . consistencies" over time (p. 257). The significance of this definition is that it broadens our view of strategy to encompass more than top management decision making. Put differently, the definition suggests that strategy results, over time, from the activities of multiple organizational actors. Thus, researchers interested in studying strategy need not limit themselves to studying the thoughts and decisions of senior managers. To discover strategy, they can also study actual firm behavior.

Mintzberg's theory allows for the thinking part of strategy in what he referred to as "intention." All strategies are at least somewhat intentional because, without intention, it is unlikely that there would be a pattern or consistency to behavior. Another component of strategy, however, is emergent. Emergent strategy is a pattern that is realized without intentions, without being anticipated in the thinking of top management, or perhaps, *despite* it. Thus, the concept of realized strategy can be broken down into intentions that lead to deliberate strategy, intentions that lead to unrealized strategy (i.e., ideas that fail to be implemented), and emergent strategies that develop as part of the pattern but without being intentional a priori.

Using this simple and highly researchable model, Mintzberg and Waters (1985) identified eight types of strategy that represented various combinations of deliberate and emergent components and discussed the contexts in which they had observed these forms of strategy in their research. It is important to recognize that all eight represent "mixed modes." Purely deliberate and purely emergent forms, while conceivable, are impossible as a practical matter. Without some kind of intention, and therefore some element of deliberate strategy, there would be no pattern. Put differently, purely emergent actions are unlikely to be consistent, absent any overarching logic or intent. Alternatively, no amount of planning and control can perfectly impose deliberate strategy onto organization behavior. It is difficult, if not impossible, to imagine a situation in which every contingency has been considered and all discretion has been eliminated from the behavior of organization members. Thus, purely deliberate forms are also ruled out.

To make the point another way, Mintzberg and Waters (1985) observe that most organizations conform in some sense to an "umbrella" form of strategy. The umbrella is one of the eight archetypes and also a metaphor for all strategy. Umbrella strategies are characterized by having a defined set of boundaries or guidelines established by top managers within which others in the organization can take some initiative. Thus, "in no organization can the central leadership totally pre-empt the discretion of others ... [and] in none does a central leadership defer totally to others" (Mintzberg & Waters, 1985, p. 263).

Nonetheless, there remains in Mintzberg's model a strong sense of hierarchical ordering, and in that light, the theory recapitulates and elaborates the concept of bounded rationality at a more collective, organizational level, rather than at the level of the individual or TMT. The hierarchical principle is manifest in each of the eight configurations. The criteria that rank alternative courses of action and create the pattern in strategy are formed and controlled by the following:

1. The goals of top management (planned strategy)
2. The vision of the entrepreneur (entrepreneurial strategy)
3. The values and beliefs of the ideology (ideological strategy)
4. The influence of the central leadership over organizational processes, such as staffing and structure (process strategy)
5. The influence of subunit leadership (unconnected strategies—not ordered in the aggregate but intentional individually)
6. The collective consensus that emerges over time (consensus strategy—deliberate after the fact)
7. An environmental force or forces that impose a strategy from the outside (imposed strategy—take away choice only in the sense that it eliminates alternatives)
8. An "umbrella" concept in which leadership defines the constraints

Even though the principle of hierarchical preference ordering remains, Mintzberg's concept of emergent strategy challenges the assumptions that strategic thinking and influence are located strictly at the top of the organizational hierarchy. In many ways, their definition and illustration of strategy anticipated and helped to stimulate the current interest in learning as a way to formulate strategy. In complex, dynamic environments, managers may create strategy by trying something, seeing what works, and only then formalizing it as an intentional direction. Still, Mintzberg and Waters (1985) close the discussion of their model with a bow to top management control:

> We wish to emphasize that emergent strategy does not have to mean that management is out of control, only—in some cases at least—that it is open, flexible and responsive.... Such behavior is especially important when an environment is too unstable or complex to comprehend.... Emergent strategy also enables a management that cannot be close enough to a situation, or to know enough about the varied activities of its organization, to surrender control to those who have the information current and detailed enough to shape realistic strategies. (p. 271)

Taking a somewhat normative tone, the authors seem to be encouraging top managers to give up control in order to retain it, to decentralize strategy as a means to gather more information, but not to cede responsibility for shaping strategic direction. Thus, although the model represents a path-breaking contribution to strategic management, in many respects it retains the assumptions of earlier work.

Autonomous Strategic Behavior

A second key milestone in the evolution toward a midlevel perspective was contributed by Robert Burgelman (1983b). Overstating it slightly, Burgelman's analysis of Chandler's (1962) case data led him to conclude just the opposite of what Chandler himself had concluded. The analysis in the original work begins with the observation that the complexities brought on by the growth of large multiproduct firms create a control crisis for top managers. Essentially, top managers are seen as being held hostage to the information and alternative solutions that lie at middle and operating levels. For Chandler, the multidivisional (M-form) structure, however, put top managers back in control; hence Chandler's famous dictum that structure follows strategy.

For Burgelman, however, the main lesson from Chandler's work was the fact that alternative strategies for change emanated from middle and operating levels. Quoting Chandler to make the point, Burgelman notes, "The initial awareness of the structural inadequacies caused by the new complexity came from executives . . . who were not themselves in a position to make organization changes" (as cited in Burgelman, 1983b, p. 63). In effect, Burgelman turns Chandler's view upside-down.

Relying on his analysis of Chandler, the work of Joseph Bower (1970, 1974), and his own clinical research, Burgelman (1983b, 1983c) developed a model of the strategic process that integrates both the top-down and bottom-up views of strategic decision making. He argues that the complexities of large multidivisional firms demand a "less-heroic" view of top managers' ability to formulate the content of strategy. Given this, his model is intended to provide more definition to what Bower and Doz (1979) identified as a new role for top management, that is, managing the strategic process rather than formulating strategy content.

The framework within which Burgelman conceptualizes strategy is drawn from the selection-variation-retention cycle of evolutionary theory (Aldrich, 1979). In contrast to population ecologists, who argue that objective environmental conditions are the principal determinant of organizational survival (Hannan & Freeman, 1977), Burgelman argues that the environment is socially constructed within the organization—that decision makers effectively enact the parameters of the situation facing them (Weick, 1979). Moreover, by accumulating "slack" resources (Bourgeois, 1980), large organizations are able to achieve a degree of independence from the pressures of external selection. Rather than being at the mercy of evolutionary forces, large firms are themselves a source of "internal" variation. Indeed, the generation of new organizational forms in response to external opportunity is a principal goal of the strategic process.

More broadly, Burgelman defines strategy making as consisting of two subprocesses. First, there is an induced loop in which responses to opportunities are enacted from the categories already contemplated by the current strategy. Second, there is an autonomous loop in which entrepreneurial initiatives are pursued by lower-level managers in response to opportunities enacted from new categories that are not contemplated by the existing strategy. The interaction of these two loops with the concept of corporate strategy (i.e., "deliberate strategy" in Mintzberg's terms) is mediated by what Burgelman refers to as the structural and strategic context.

By definition, autonomous strategic behavior develops outside of the structural context—that is, apart from the organization's formal administrative arrangements (structure, control system, incentives, etc.). It occurs because certain "strategically inclined" operating-level actors see the resources created by the corporate form as a means to pursue opportunity. Given sufficient autonomy and a pool of unused resources, these internal entrepreneurs express the same instincts for growth as entrepreneurs outside the corporation do.

To be useful to the corporation, however, autonomous initiatives ultimately must be accepted as part of the official strategy. This occurs through the efforts of middle managers who manipulate the strategic context. Using political mechanisms, middle managers question the current concept of strategy and provide top management with a "retrospective rationalization" that permits executives to accept autonomous strategic behavior. In effect, middle managers shield autonomous behavior from the formal controls and sanctions of the structural context, thereby allowing divergent initiative to seep into the corporate strategy.

The work of top managers, according to Burgelman (1983a), is to avoid the natural tendency to overcontrol—that is, to design the organization so that it encourages rather than suppresses entrepreneurship. It is in the discussion of this point, however, that Burgelman's top management orientation shows itself: "From the perspective of top management, guarding the firm against narrowly self-centered opportunism . . . is a special problem in relationship to autonomous strategic behavior" (1983a, p. 1361). Given the inability of the structural context to create entrepreneurial behavior, Burgelman urges top management to cultivate a group of middle-level managers who can think strategically. These middle-level managers must be allowed to challenge the current strategy, and top managers need to adopt a tolerance for ambiguity and a "wait and see" attitude toward the evolving strategic vision. Still, although "top management cannot understand the strategy completely either, [it] should be capable of sustaining a higher rate of progress [than middle- or operating-level managers sustain] in understanding [strategy] as it unfolds" (1983a, p. 1361).

In later research, Burgelman (1991, 1994) is more explicit about how top management can manage the strategic process. On the basis of a longitudinal field study of Intel Corporation, he proposes that successful firms simultaneously maintain top-down strategic intent and bottom-up experimentation and selection processes (1991, p. 256). In addition, selection can be managed in the induced loop through administrative mechanisms and cultural influencing so that the process reflects external selection processes. A key part of this is creating an atmosphere of "constructive confrontation" in which ideas can be challenged on the basis of fact and subjected to debate and objective analysis. "The data suggest that the influence of top management in strategy making was undeniably very strong, but that there was also a perception . . . that, most of the time, knowledge and facts tend to win over positional power" (Burgelman, 1991, p. 252).

Thus, in this distinctly bottom-up, evolutionary model, which explicitly acknowledges the value of knowledge at operating levels, strategy making is a process that is characterized by the use of rational processes and hierarchical preference ordering. Moreover, top managers are clearly viewed as the source of strategic, as opposed to technical, knowledge and as the center of the organization's social network.

Strategy Making as Organizational Capability

Stuart Hart's (1992) paper is an important synthesis and integration of various typologies of strategy making (Brodwin & Bourgeois, 1984; Burgelman, 1983b; Mintzberg & Waters, 1985) that have appeared in the literature. From these, he identifies somewhat overlapping dimensions and distills three critical elements of strategy making: rationality, vision, and involvement. He develops his own comprehensive typology based on these, which is then supported in subsequent research (Hart & Banbury, 1994). Hart's five types of strategy-making process are command, symbolic, rational, transactive, and generative. He differentiates these modes in terms of variations in the roles played by top management and other organization members.

The key insight provided by this work is the recognition that strategy making itself is a critical capability that helps determine organizational success or failure (Hart & Banbury, 1994). The typology draws connections between various environmental contexts, needed strategizing modes, and organizational performance. Most fundamentally, Hart observes that, for successful adaptation and sustained performance, organizations must be able to use a variety of strategy-making modes. Furthermore, firms that can use distal modes (i.e., have the broadest

Table 2.2   Key Insights in the Move Toward a Midlevel Perspective

Author	Insight
Mintzberg and Waters (1985)	Strategy as a pattern in a stream of actions. Recognizes that strategy results from more than the decisions of top managers. Strategy evolves over time from the activities of multiple organizational actors.
Burgelman (1983b, 1983c)	Strategic behaviors are both induced and autonomous. Individuals within the organization may act outside the "umbrella."
Hart (1992)	Strategy making is a capability that influences organizational performance. Firms need to enlist a variety of strategy-making modes to be successful.

array of strategy-making capability) have the best chance for continued success.

Table 2.2 summarizes the key insights contributed by Mintzberg and by Burgelman and the integration offered by Hart. The next chapter builds on these and begins to outline the key assumptions underlying a midlevel view of strategy making. Before concluding, however, the remainder of this chapter describes our own work, placing it within the context of the field's overall evolution.

The Evolution of Our Own Thinking

In 1987, we became interested in how agreement on strategy among members of the top management team influenced organizational performance. Research by Bourgeois (1980, 1985), Grinyer and Norburn (1977-1978), and Dess (1987) had produced an equivocal set of findings. Oversimplifying a bit, some studies found a positive relationship between consensus and performance, some found no relationship, and some found a negative relationship.

Several things could account for the inconsistent findings in top management team consensus research, and a number of papers (Bowman & Ambrosini, 1997; Dess & Priem, 1995; Markoczy, 1997; Priem, 1992; Wooldridge & Floyd, 1989) have addressed the issue of antecedent conditions and contingencies that affect the consensus-performance link. Our own thinking led us to conclude that the relationship between consensus and performance might be dependent significantly on the scope of such agreement—that is, who was included in the definition of strategic consensus (Wooldridge & Floyd, 1989).

The original argument for a consensus-performance link was that agreement among top managers about strategies and goals would create improved integration and coordination in the activities of other organizational members (Bourgeois, 1980; Dess & Origer, 1987). Greater consistency in action would lead to more efficient implementation and improved performance. Put differently, if TMT consensus leads to coherent organizational arrangements (e.g., structure, control systems, etc.), the behavior of other organization members will be more likely to conform to top management thinking.

As a not-so-subtle reflection of the "thinking versus doing" dichotomy (Mintzberg, 1990), this assumption prevented researchers from considering how the cognitions of other organization actors might affect organization behavior. Even if the structure and control system encouraged appropriate activity, more efficient implementation of the strategy might not occur unless organization members at multiple levels in the organization understood the strategy (cognitively) and were committed to it (affectively; Dess, 1987; Wooldridge & Floyd, 1989). Misunderstanding and low commitment could result (a) if the strategy had not been effectively communicated and organization members therefore misunderstood it (i.e., if they were ill informed) or (b) if they understood it but believed it was infeasible or otherwise ill advised (i.e., if they were skeptical; Floyd & Wooldridge, 1992). As Dess (1987) argued, understanding and commitment are independent dimensions of consensus; thus, managers might even be committed to a strategy that they did not understand. We referred to this third possibility as "blind devotion" (Floyd & Wooldridge, 1992).

In the face of any of these circumstances, there would be little reason to expect more consistency in realized strategy or improved organizational performance to result from TMT consensus. Indeed, Guth and MacMillan (1986) had already shown that when middle managers were uncommitted to a strategy, the results could include foot dragging, overt noncompliance, and sabotage. In our own interviews with managers, we found that such resistance was often the result of middle management's sincere belief that the strategy was not in the organization's interest. Apparently even more common, however, many middle managers did not have a clue about top management's priorities. Large sample surveys by the Gallup organization and the American Management Association suggested that 60% or more of middle managers did not understand organizational strategy.[1] Thus, there were reasons to suspect that researchers' limited view of the scope of consensus had produced the conflicting findings.

These concerns led us to middle management. We initiated a study on consensus among middle-level managers (Wooldridge & Floyd, 1990). In particular, we wanted to study both dimensions of consensus (understanding and commitment) among middle managers with respect to the deliberate strategy of top management. We reasoned that an important antecedent of consensus among middle managers was their involvement in the strategy process. That is, unless they had participated in strategy making at some level, it would be unlikely that middle managers would either understand or be committed to the intended strategy. We measured five forms of involvement: involvement in defining objectives, generating options, evaluating options, developing details, and taking necessary action.

Furthermore, as shown in Figure 2.2, our research model posited two possible "paths" through which middle management involvement might improve organizational performance: (a) Their involvement could improve the quality of strategic decisions and hence organizational performance, or (b) their involvement could improve commitment to deliberate strategy, more efficient implementation, and hence organizational performance. The latter hypothesis represented our interpretation of the traditional argument for a TMT consensus-performance relationship (Wooldridge & Floyd, 1990).

Our findings were somewhat surprising. First, in partialling out the influence of middle managers' involvement on performance, we found evidence that the effect of "improved decision making" (Path A in Figure 2.2) was stronger than the effect of "improved implementation" (Path B). When middle managers were involved in setting goals and generating alternatives, we found a greater performance effect than when they were involved purely in the implementation side of the process. Second, although greater involvement produced higher levels of consensus among middle managers, this increased consensus was not

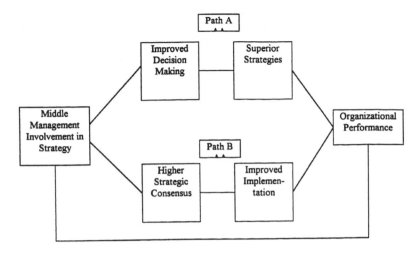

Figure 2.2. Theoretical Model of Middle Management Involvement in Strategy
SOURCE: Adapted from Wooldridge and Floyd (1990).

related to organizational performance. That is, the hypothesized links in Path B did not appear in our data. In particular, higher strategic consensus did not seem to produce improved implementation.

We measured middle management consensus as the sum of collective differences between members of a middle management cohort and the priorities expressed by the chief executive. This approach was consistent with the purely cognitive definition of consensus used at the time. In retrospect, however, the fact that we did not measure the affective or commitment side of the construct may explain the failure to find a statistical association between consensus and performance.

Overall, the message from this study seemed to be that middle management played a significant role in developing strategy and that the effects of its substantive contribution could be detected in large-sample, statistical research. Although Mintzberg and Burgelman had argued respectively for the importance of emergent and autonomous strategic behavior in dynamic environments, neither had published evidence for this effect in a broad sample of firms. Our study (Wooldridge & Floyd, 1990), however, suggested that the effect might be more widespread—not limited to technologically intensive (Burgelman, 1983c, 1991, 1994, 1996) or professionally oriented organizations (Mintzberg, Raisinghani, & Theoret, 1976).

	Upward	Downward
Divergent	Championing	Facilitating
Integrative	Synthesizing	Implementing

Figure 2.3. Middle Manager Roles in Strategy
SOURCE: Adapted from Floyd and Wooldridge (1992).

Thus, we set out to identify the strategic roles of middle management, develop an instrument that would measure these roles, and examine their effects on the substantive strategy of the firm (Floyd & Wooldridge, 1992). In specifying the strategic roles of middle management, we took our cue from Burgelman's admonition that strategic behavior can be defined as the interaction of cognition and action and that the strategy process requires both order and diversity. This suggested dividing middle management's strategic role into its cognitive and behavioral elements. On the cognitive dimension, we identified a diversity-producing and an order-producing component. On the behavioral dimension, middle management's influence was conceptualized as upward- and downward-directed.

This reasoning left us with a classic, four-cell matrix, and to label the cells, we turned to the rich clinical descriptions of middle management activity found in Bower (1970), Burgelman (1983c), Kanter (1983), and Kidder (1981). Culling this literature and the descriptions of middle management in the strategy implementation literature (especially Nutt, 1987) not only produced tentative labels for the cells in our matrix (see Figure 2.3) but also led to the development of 21 descriptions of specific activities.

Using these descriptions as the basis for a questionnaire, we collected data from 259 middle managers in 25 organizations (details of the methodology can be found in Floyd and Wooldridge, 1992). An exploratory factor analysis suggested revisions to our original expectations about how the items would relate to the four roles in our typology, but, ultimately, we refined the instrument so that it contained measures of the strategic roles in the typology.[2] Then we compared the levels of the roles for cohorts of middle managers with measures of the organization's strategic orientation, such as defender, analyzer, or prospector (Miles & Snow, 1978). We found that, consistent with our hypotheses, the implementation role was the highest of the four roles across all three orientations. More interestingly, prospecting firms reported higher levels of championing than managers in defenders and higher levels of facilitating than managers in both analyzers and defenders (Floyd & Wooldridge, 1992, p. 164).

This study represented a small breakthrough in our thinking about the strategy process. In the 1990 study, we compared the understandings of middle managers with those of the chief executive officer and measured the involvement of middle managers in the traditional five-stage model of strategy. This approach clearly put middle management behavior in the context of a process that is defined with top management at the center. In the 1992 study, however, we conceptualized middle management's involvement in a way that decoupled it from a rational, top-down decision process. Moreover, we found evidence that patterns in this kind of middle management strategic behavior were related to the realization of organizational strategy. Thus, we had stepped just outside the dominant assumptions in the field, and in the process, we found tentative evidence in support of a midlevel perspective on strategy.

As we continued to examine midlevel involvement in strategy, we began to suspect that the relationship between middle managers' strategic behavior and organizational performance was not linear. To explore this suspicion, we drew from Burgelman's intraorganizational ecology model and developed three new hypotheses. First, we argued that boundary-spanning positions give managers increased opportunity to mediate between the internal and external selection environments, and this promotes higher levels of upward influence activity. Second, we predicted that variety (literally, variance across a cohort group) in the pattern of upward influence represented a pattern likely to be adaptive in the face of changing strategic issues, and thus deduced that variation would be associated with higher performance. Finally, we hypothesized the reverse for downward influence—that consistency (either all high or all low levels of strategic behavior) in the pattern of downward influence provided the needed balance of control and flexibility associated with the implementation of a particular strategy. Thus, consistency of downward influence and variation in upward influence would be associated with higher levels of organizational performance. Using independent measures of performance and middle management behavior, we found that the statistical results were supportive (Floyd & Wooldridge, 1997).

Conclusion

In our minds, the relationship between middle management strategic behavior and organizational performance provides the impetus for adopting a deliberately middle-level perspective in strategy research. After all, few studies of top management behavior have been able to make such direct links to the bottom line. Thus, in 1994 and 1995, we undertook a book-length treatment of these ideas (Floyd & Wooldridge, 1996). One result was that we came to a greater appreciation for the link between middle-level activity, organizational capability, and competitive advantage. Indeed, the resource-based view provided the conceptual framework for our conclusions.

Writing the book also led to a number of consulting engagements in which we worked with top- and middle-level managers to enhance the quantity and quality of strategic involvement. We learned many things from these experiences, not all of them confirming our theories. Still, one thing that impressed us was the universality of the feeling that top managers were simply no longer in a position to make strategic decisions on their own (if they ever were) and that middle-level managers, in particular, should take on a more substantive role in defining strategy. In no case can we claim that managers in client organizations took a middle-level view of strategy making. As with researchers, our clients' view of strategy reflected the assumptions embedded in a top management perspective. We think this view is as much a limitation to the practice of strategic management as it is to research.

The premises of our 1996 book were framed in a capability-based view of strategy. This same notion of competitive advantage is the premise for the midlevel view traced here. In the next chapter, we show why a midlevel perspective is necessary to understand the processes organizations use to renew and develop organization capabilities. On the basis of this argument, we offer an alternative set of assumptions about the strategy process. These provide both boundaries to our subsequent theorizing and guideposts for an expanded discussion of process (in Chapters 4 and 5) that embraces the middle of the organization.

Notes

1. Gallup poll reported in *Fortune,* December 4, 1989, p. 58, and supported by research by D. M. Reid (1989) "Operationalizing Strategic Planning," *Strategic Management Journal, 10,* 553-567. American Management Association survey with similar findings reported in the *Wall Street Journal,* July 5, 1995, p. 1.

2. As might be expected, the measures were less than perfect, and low reliabilities for the synthesizing and facilitating roles, in particular, provide a limitation to our findings.

3　Toward a Middle-Level View

Developing New Assumptions

This important difference in occupation means that the top management perspective is useful in studying resource deployment processes but is limiting to researchers who want to study capability accumulation or the process of how an organization "learns to do new things" (Nelson, 1991). We believe the latter requires a middle-level perspective.

The preceding chapter described a growing recognition of the importance of middle-level strategic behavior in strategy process research and also highlighted three assumptions that continue to dominate the field: (a) Strategy making is a choice process involving the hierarchical ordering of alternatives; (b) top managers encounter and process the information necessary to make a choice; and (c) the choice made by top management leads directly to organizational outcomes. In this chapter, we draw from the literature on the resource-based view (RBV) of the firm to identify how these assumptions have limited the field's scope of inquiry and therefore our understanding of how strategy develops in complex organizations. We then offer a set of alternative assumptions meant to guide and shape research from a middle-level perspective.

All theory requires boundary-setting assumptions to delineate the context in which the theory applies (Bacharach, 1989; Dubin, 1976). Seen in this light, the three assumptions identified above provide needed definition to the scope of the strategy process. Researchers'

Table 3.1   Differentiating the Top Management Perspective From the
            Middle-Level Perspective

Problem	Key Actors	Process Mechanisms	Economic Orientation
Helping top managers analyze conditions and formulate strategy	Top management team	Analysis, decision making, and consensus	Industrial organization theory
Developing organizational capabilities	Middle-level managers	Learning, network development, and trust	Resource-based

awareness of these conditions—either explicit or implicit—has been useful in building a cumulative stream of research.[1] Indeed, in this sense, the assumptions have been extremely functional.

By highlighting the assumptions of the top management perspective, then, we are not asserting that they are "wrong" or inappropriate. Rather, our claim is that, like all assumptions, these have simplified, and thereby partitioned out, some phenomena of interest. Stated differently, our critique of the top management perspective is focused not on what we have learned but on what we *haven't learned*. Thus, our call for a middle-level perspective in strategy research is meant to complement, not replace, existing theory and knowledge. Perhaps more to the point, a middle-level perspective makes sense only insofar as it is juxtaposed against the top management perspective. By making explicit the shift in assumptions, constructs, and relationships required for the new perspective, future research in this stream can both inform and be informed by research in the other stream. There may be contradictions and inconsistencies between the two perspectives, but we think a constructive approach will contribute to better research.[2] Table 3.1 summarizes what we think are key differences between the top management perspective and the emerging, middle-level perspective.

Rethinking Vertical Relationships in the Strategy Process

The central argument in this chapter is that, mainly by virtue of its boundary-setting assumptions, the top management perspective is unable to provide information on certain essential features of the strategy process. More specifically, although the top management perspective tells us a great deal about the processes organizations use to allocate and deploy resources, it tells us much less about processes related to the accumulation of resources and the development of capabilities. Said in other words, the top management perspective helps us understand processes associated with the "cross-sectional" problem of positioning the firm within its product-market environment. It says less, however, about the "longitudinal problem" of building capabilities and sustaining competitive advantage (Porter, 1991).

In brief, our argument begins with the proposal that middle-level managers are uniquely positioned between top management priorities and operating realities. Many people in the middle of the organization also gain a keen sense of the environmental context, through exposure to customers, suppliers, professional associations, and so forth (Dutton, Ashford, O'Neill, Hayes, & Wierba, 1997; Lawrence & Lorsch, 1967). The middle level, then, is where knowledge about intention, operations, and context is most likely to come together to form a complete strategic picture (Nonaka, 1994). Social interactions at this level have a high potential to influence strategy in both upward and downward directions (Floyd & Wooldridge, 1992, 1997; Wooldridge & Floyd, 1990).

The problem of developing capabilities focuses attention on a series of "vertical relationships"—between levels of management, resources in the environment (capital, technical, and market), functional and managerial resources within the organization, short- and long-term gain, and operations and strategic intent. To study the accumulation process, therefore, the individuals, groups, and activities positioned to make these connections must become the subjects of our research. Less a focus on middle-level managers, per se, the new perspective designates a point of observation. Practically speaking, this means expanding the theoretical and empirical scope of strategy process research and focusing on managers and professionals in the middle of the organization. Equally important, it means changing our understanding of how the middle relates to other levels.

Figure 3.1 suggests the pattern of relationships between top, middle, and operating managers that we are visualizing. To illustrate the structure of these interactions, we offer the lowly trilobite, one of mother nature's most enduring creatures. Living in shallow and later deeper ocean waters, trilobites survived at least three eons of environmental

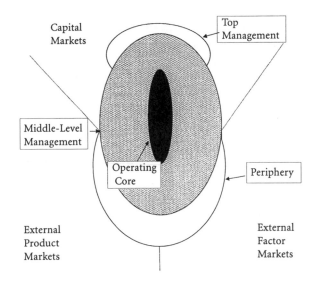

Figure 3.1. Interactions Between Top, Middle, and Operating-Level Management

variation. The structure is preserved in fossils commonly found in the United States, and its descendant, the horseshoe crab, continues as one of the most successful crustaceans on the planet.[3]

One way to understand the creature's long-term survival is to see the genius underlying the simplicity of its structure. It has a small number of minimally specialized parts that are held together by a strong middle and that interact with one another in an infinite variety of ways. It is useful to think about interactions between organizational levels in the renewal process along much the same lines.

Thus, top managers are shown not as the brain but as a distinct structure mediating between the organization and capital markets. Their role is to buffer the influence of capital markets, maintain economic discipline, and hold others accountable to stakeholders' interests. The elongated, central structure represents the operating core of the organization. The purpose here is to transform inputs into outputs. The middle level is suggested by the neuroskeletal lines of the fossil. Notice the large number of connections the middle level makes from the periphery or head of the organization into or from the operating core. This shows the great variety of possible interactions among the parts and the key mediating role of middle-level actors—transmitting knowledge and influence within the organism and thereby holding the parts together.

The trilobite provides a good metaphor because it suggests the structure of interactions among top, middle, and operating levels in the process of strategic renewal. With this image, we want to overturn the notion that the strategy process is governed entirely by an authority system or management hierarchy. There are vertical connections between the levels, and these are critical to connecting environments, resources, time frames, operations, and strategy. The interactions across these connections, however, are not premised on a strategy conceived and controlled from the top. Top managers do, of course, have a conception of strategy, but—and this is the important point—so do middle- and operating-level actors. There is intention within all parts of the system.

Despite the great variety of possible connections, the structure of a trilobite is not very complicated. Indeed, its simplicity is one of the reasons it survived so long. Parts are minimally specialized within levels to accommodate a high degree of flexibility. Between levels, relationships are highly symbiotic so that activities in the head make it possible for middle and operating levels to function, for example. The trilobite adapted not by creating entirely new structures in the face of change but by continuously combining parts of its structure in new ways. Therefore, the trilobite image suggests that renewal depends less on defining deliberate strategy and reorienting structure to fit the new direction and depends more on "combinative capability" (Kogut & Zander, 1992)—the capacity to build new capabilities by combining resources in new ways, by making new connections.

Finally, although we do not want to enter into a detailed discussion of how complexity theory may or may not apply to organizations, it is impossible to avoid the parallels between the system of interactions we are describing here and the features of *complex adaptive systems.* Waldrop (1992) offers an excellent overview of this idea as it applies to social and physical systems of all kinds. All such systems have the following properties. We believe that these apply to the system of social interactions associated with renewal in large, complex organizations.

- Control is highly dispersed, with many agents acting parallel.
- There are multiple levels of organization, with agents at one level serving as building blocks for agents at a higher level but with structural relationships subject to constant revision and rearrangement.
- A host of imperfectly smart agents behave in ways consistent with their intentions and expectations about the future.

The trilobite and complexity theory offer a description of what have been viewed historically as vertical relationships in the strategy process. Like all metaphors, ours oversimplifies reality, and, specifically, it underplays the role hierarchy. Later in the book (Chapter 6), we will become much more specific about these interactions, and at that point, we make clear that there remains a role for authority and hierarchy in the process. The main point we are trying to drive home now is that there is much more than authority to the relationships between top, middle, and operating levels. Indeed, thinking about these vertical interactions purely in terms of hierarchy interferes with a robust description of the strategic renewal process.

The rest of this chapter is meant to bring this static image alive. First, we summarize the implications of a resource- or capability-based view of competitive advantage for strategy process theory. This leads us to a metalevel process model that distinguishes two key activities of the organization—resource deployment and resource accumulation. We draw both distinctions and connections between these two. The second part of the argument links these ideas to the recent literature of strategic renewal and argues that resource deployment and accumulation are both aspects of an evolutionary change process. Finally, in the last part of the chapter, we detail our reasoning for taking a middle-level perspective, lay out a new set of assumptions for process research, and explain why the literatures of organizational knowledge, social networks, and trust are pertinent to the discussion.

Resource Deployment and Accumulation in Strategy Making

As we observed in Chapter 1, during the 1980s, research in the strategy field was occupied largely by explaining the nature of competitive strategy, or what we have identified as understanding how firms position themselves in product markets. From a process point of view, competitive positioning can be seen as involving (a) the choice of a competitive strategy that offers the greatest potential for growth and profitability with the least risk (i.e., strategy formulation) and (b) the deployment of resources for the structures, systems, and people needed to implement such a choice (i.e., strategy implementation). This description is consistent with the delineation of formulation and implementation issues in process research (e.g., Chakravarthy & Doz, 1992; Schendel & Hofer, 1979) and with descriptions in leading texts. Despite exhortations to the contrary (Mintzberg, 1990; Schendel, 1991), the formulation-implementation description remains fundamental to many—perhaps most—curricula in the field.[4]

Normative models of decision making about competitive positioning typically take into account the internal profile of the firm, thereby taking stock of its accumulated resources. This assessment is most often conceptualized as the organizational strengths and weaknesses being considered in deciding which strategy has the greatest potential for success (Andrews, 1971). As a part of such a decision-making process, strategy involves either building or reinforcing strengths and overcoming or correcting weaknesses, and to this extent, the process raises issues of developing new resources and capabilities in the short run. The "short run" means a time horizon consistent with implementing the chosen strategy.

For the most part, however, strategy process theorists prior to 1986 did not focus on the resources themselves as a source of competitive advantage. They also did not attempt to explain the processes associated with accumulating such resources. With a few notable exceptions (Hrebiniak & Snow, 1982; Lippman & Rumelt, 1982; Nelson & Winter, 1982; Penrose, 1959; Wernerfelt, 1984), competitive advantage was seen to derive from a firm's strategic position (Porter, 1980). The positioning view of strategy focuses on the allocation of resources—not their accumulation—and such allocations typically require top management approval. Thus, positioning leads rather directly to a view of process that puts top management at the center. In short, theorists have been interested in how resources are allocated in support of a competitive positioning strategy, and this has led to an emphasis on top managers as the locus of strategy making.

Strategy as Accumulating Resources and Sustaining Competitive Advantage

Jay Barney (1986, 1991) is most often credited with redirecting attention toward firm resources, rather than or in addition to strategic position, as a source of competitive advantage. According to the resource-based view, sustained competitive advantage results from the ownership and control of resources that are rare, valued by the market, nontradable, nonsubstitutable, and difficult or impossible to imitate. Such resources include, and very often combine, physical assets, intangible resources, and organizational capabilities. Thus, for example, the key resources underlying Walt Disney Company's competitive advantage are its animated characters. But these assets would be of far less value in the absence of Disney's ability to produce universal and timeless entertainment, whether in theme parks or animated films.

Disney's capability is an example of what Leonard-Barton (1992) calls a core capability: "the knowledge set that distinguishes [the firm] and provides a competitive advantage" (p. 113). Other labels given to this concept include distinctive competence (Snow & Hrebiniak, 1980) and core competencies (Prahalad & Hamel, 1990). The importance of such a concept has been recognized for some time in the strategy literature. In 1974, for example, Rumelt found that diversification strategies that leveraged an existing skill base were associated with higher performance than strategies that strayed into areas requiring different core skills. In recent literature, the discussion of core capabilities has focused on an organization's ability to learn new capabilities, or its dynamic capability (Nelson, 1991; Teece, Pisano, & Shuen, 1997), and indeed the question of *how an organization accumulates new capabilities* is the principal focus of this book.

To date, only a handful of researchers have taken up the challenge represented in this question. We will discuss the literature that exists in the following section, but it is interesting to pause and consider why there is so little.

Besides the assumptions of the top management perspective already identified, there are at least two other reasons that may account for the strategy field's apparent neglect of resource accumulation and capability development processes. First, the description of resources and the accumulation process in economic theory tends to emphasize features that discourage systematic study. Organizational capabilities are defined as socially complex combinations of assets, technologies, and organizational routines (Barney, 1991; Nelson, 1991). They are said to be idiosyncratic and infinite in their variety. More to the point, they develop "inside the 'black box' of the firm" (Collis, 1994, p. 145).

For example, Barney explains that information asymmetries in factor markets must exist for firms to enjoy superior resource configurations. He traces the source of such differences to conditions that are idiosyncratic at the firm level and, in particular, to *luck* (Barney, 1991).

Similarly, Dierickx and Cool (1989) argue that the accumulation of valuable capabilities is idiosyncratic and path-dependent. Reed and DeFillippi (1990) maintain, for these and other reasons, that the relationship between firm-level capabilities and competitive advantage is "causally ambiguous." It must be said that these arguments seem necessary to account for the inimitability of capabilities, a key requirement if they are to be the basis of sustainable competitive advantage (Peteraf, 1993). Still, what kind of generalizable theory, much less empirical research, can explain an inherently idiosyncratic, complex, causally ambiguous process?

Second, strategy process research to date seems not to have recognized the distinction between processes related to the *deployment* of capabilities and processes related to the *accumulation* of capabilities. Capability deployment is a decision-making process that takes firm assets and capabilities (i.e., its resources) as givens. The purpose is to decide how and where to position the firm.[5] Capability accumulation, on the other hand, is the process that leads to the development of socially complex bundles of firm assets and capabilities, some of which may become the basis for competitive advantage (Barney, 1991).

Put differently, capability accumulation focuses on the input or factor-market side of the transformation process, whereas capability deployment focuses on the output or product-market side of the transformation process. The latter seems transparently strategic because it involves decisions that affect the firm's competitive position. The former is much more amorphous, however. It involves decisions and actions, such as the acquisition of ordinary assets, day-to-day learning, and so forth, that are not ordinarily considered strategic. Like the characterizations provided by economic arguments, this description suggests a set of phenomena that is difficult to isolate as part of a strategic process.

To focus on the distinction between capability accumulation and deployment, Figure 3.2 depicts a metalevel model of strategy making. The figure shows the outcomes of the strategy process as the firm's competitive position (Porter, 1980) and its resource base (Wernerfelt, 1984). The former results from decisions to deploy resources in the value chain of activities that make up the firm (Porter, 1985). The latter results from the historical accumulation of resources that support competitive positions (Dierickx & Cool, 1989). Competitive advantage and economic performance result from the combination of a viable com-

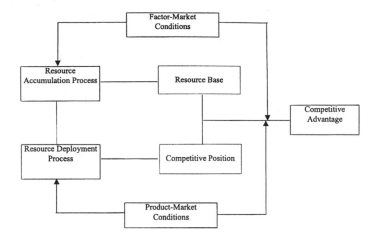

Figure 3.2. A Metalevel Model of Strategy-Making Processes

petitive position and a unique, nontradable, nonsubstitutable, and in-imitable resource base (Barney, 1991; Peteraf, 1993).

It is important to note that the deployment and accumulation processes occur over different time horizons. Deployment requires the time it takes to put existing resources into place to support the currently chosen strategy (with, as noted above, incremental investments to reinforce strengths or overcome weaknesses). Accumulation, on the other hand, requires the time it takes to acquire or develop capabilities, combine them with other resources, and learn how to use them. In the case of organizational capabilities such as Disney's ability to entertain, the time horizon may be several decades. Because it is impossible to know so far in advance what specific capabilities may be needed, the decisions associated with accumulating capabilities are guided only by broad visions or "strategic intent" (Hamel & Prahalad, 1989). Inevitably, many of the "flow" decisions that lead to the accumulation of capability "stocks" (Dierickx & Cool, 1989) are made on the basis of "intelligent guesses" and are informed very little by the current strategy (Hamel & Prahalad, 1989).

Moreover, although strategy making continuously iterates between accumulation and deployment, conceptually at least, an organization must have accumulated capabilities before it can deploy them. The two processes come together when existing resources are being deployed in support of existing strategies (i.e., when decision makers are solving the cross-sectional problem) and when future capabilities are being contemplated in light of future strategies (when decision makers are solving the longitudinal problem). Uncertainty exists at either of these points of convergence, but it looms much larger in the longitudinal problem because there is uncertainty about which strategy will be appropriate in the future as well as which capabilities will be required to support it.

The asynchronous nature of accumulation and deployment processes—that is, the problem that capabilities must be accumulated before the strategy is known—led Cool and Schendel (1987) to identify the concept of strategic risk. Strategic risk is uncertainty over whether the firm will have the critical resources needed to support a given strategy. The sources of uncertainty include conditions in output and factor markets and the resource needs of a given position.

The purpose of Figure 3.2 is not to impose another convenient dichotomy onto strategy process theory. In fact, we would agree with those who point out that a resource-based explanation of strategy is inherently dynamic (Porter, 1991; Teece et al., 1997). The accumulation and deployment processes are two sides of a learning loop that is at the core of explaining how competitive advantage develops, a point that we reconsider in the discussion of strategic renewal later in this chapter.

Our immediate purpose in differentiating these two subprocesses is to suggest that their locus within the organization may be different. That is, the knowledge and behavior most closely associated with resource deployment and resource accumulation, respectively, can be found at different levels in the organizational hierarchy. Deployment occurs predominantly at the top. This is not to say that middle managers are never involved in deployment. Bower (1970) describes several examples of middle managers circumventing formal channels to secure resources and enter new markets. Accumulation, on the other hand, occurs predominantly at the middle, although top managers may also be involved in accumulation processes.[6] This important difference in occupation means that the top management perspective is useful in studying resource deployment processes but is limiting to researchers who want to study capability accumulation or the process of how an organization "learns to do new things" (Nelson, 1991). We believe the latter requires a middle-level perspective.

Before turning to a specific justification for a middle-level perspective, however, we need to focus more precisely on the process of developing new capabilities. The capability development process has already been described by a number of authors under the name "strategic renewal." In the next section, we describe this literature and point out what we believe are its current limitations. We see these limitations as opportunities to develop new theory. The following discussion, therefore, provides a conceptual framework for depicting the potential contribution of a middle-level perspective to developing a new theory of strategic renewal.

The Concept of Strategic Renewal

The term *strategic renewal* has come to be identified with evolutionary models of strategic change (Barnett & Burgelman, 1996; Burgelman, 1983c; Grinyer & Spender, 1979; Nelson & Winter, 1982). Theorists who use the term assume that strategic change grows out of the current situation, that it is accomplished over time, and that it is continuous. Huff, Huff, and Thomas (1992), for example, describe the "evolution of strategic renewal" as the interaction between the forces of organizational "stress and inertia." Similarly, Barr, Stimpert, and Huff (1992) focus on top managers' mental models and describe renewal in terms of managers' "incremental reassessments" of the relationship between environmental change and organizational performance. In these and other similar models of renewal, *evolutionary* generally means that the pattern of change is incremental (Braybrooke & Lindblom, 1963; Quinn, 1980) and that change is created by an iterative cycle of belief, action, and learning (Barr et al., 1992; Doz, 1996; Huff et al., 1992; Johnson, 1987).

Burgelman's (1983b, 1991, 1994, 1996) conceptualization, of course, goes further than this. As we noted in the previous chapter, he explicitly frames renewal in terms of the variation-selection-retention framework from general evolutionary theory and thereby adopts the tenets of population ecology (Aldrich, 1979; Hannan & Freeman, 1977) for the intraorganizational environment. For Burgelman (1991), escape from the forces of *external* environmental selection is possible only if the *internal* selection environment generates a sufficient variety of autonomous strategic initiatives. This involves experimentation at operating levels, the development of new skills, and the exploration of new market opportunities. Whether such initiatives develop, then, depends on the willingness of middle-level managers to provide "seed" resources and to champion specific proposals coming out of the initiative to top management. Autonomous strategic initiatives thereby provide "early warning signals" of significant environmental change. Successful adaptation, however, still requires that top management recognize which initiatives should become part of the organization's official strategy.

Thus, Burgelman's concept of renewal (1991, 1994, 1996) departs significantly from prior theory on strategic change from the top management perspective (e.g., Carter, 1971; Child, 1972; Hambrick & Mason, 1984). He argues explicitly that major "strategic change may take place before it is recognized or acknowledged as such by top management" (Burgelman, 1996, p. 209). Indeed, on the induced side of strategy, top managers are a primary source of inertia (Alrdich, 1979). They may induce relatively minor adjustments in strategy by articulating a vision or applying structural and process mechanisms, such as strategic planning. When top managers attempt to induce major strategic change, however, they usually redefine the organization's domain, thereby effectively renouncing the learning accumulated within the organization. This kind of reorientation exposes the organization to very significant risks (March, 1981; Singh, 1986), increases its vulnerability to external selection pressures, and reduces its chances for survival.

Reorientation in the form of a domain shift is not likely to result from the autonomous loop, Burgelman (1991) argues, because autonomous strategic behavior evolves out of existing competencies and leads to incremental learning. To the extent that the successful "reorientations" described by Tushman and Romanelli (1985) are even possible, they are preceded by renewal activities (i.e., bottom-up learning). Burgelman reserves the concept of strategic renewal exclusively for processes that involve evolutionary change in core competencies that is initiated by learning at lower levels of the organizational hierarchy.

Our own definition is broader than Burgelman's. *Strategic renewal is a managerial process associated with promoting and accommodating new knowledge and innovative behavior that results in change in an organization's product-market strategy and/or its core capabilities* (Burgelman, 1991; Huff et al., 1992; Hurst, Rush, & White, 1989). This definition expands the concept of strategic renewal to include change in domain (i.e., product-market strategy) or in strategic positioning as well as change in core capabilities. There are three principal reasons for our approach.

First, this definition resonates with the resource-based view of strategy (Barney, 1991; Conner, 1991). The RBV holds that a firm's long-run competitiveness is determined by the dynamic fit between resources, including organizational capabilities, and the competitive environment (Nelson, 1991; Teece et al., 1997). A firm accumulates resources, or develops new capabilities, through historical, path-dependent interactions with factor and product markets as it seeks distinctive ways to create customer value or to deliver value efficiently (Dierickx & Cool, 1989; Grant, 1991; Prahalad & Hamel, 1990). As noted earlier, this "longitudinal" explanation of how competitive advantage develops complements the "cross-sectional" view that it results from allocating resources to protect privileged industry positions (Porter, 1991).

Accordingly, a theory of strategic renewal must recognize that maintaining adaptiveness requires both exploiting existing capabilities and exploring new ones and—more important—that these two facets of organizational learning are fundamentally inseparable (Levinthal & March, 1993). Put differently, as top managers direct the deployment of existing capabilities and other resources to expand or defend a competitive position, they influence the context for experimentation and entrepreneurship at middle and operating levels of the organization. Bottom-up initiatives may be autonomous in the sense that they are not induced by the formal organizational structure or control systems, but they occur in a market and technological context that is shaped by the current strategy.

Second, a broad definition is useful because it provides a foundation for a more holistic theory of the renewal process. Too often, theories of strategy development have been created piecemeal, based on what have proved to be troublesome distinctions such as formulation and implementation. Chakravarthy and Doz (1992) note the "compartmentalized view that characterizes much [of strategy process] research" (p. 9). They call for theory that integrates recent conceptual developments in the field (e.g., strategic intent, core capability, renewal) with the administrative systems and managerial behaviors required to support such concepts. Accordingly, our definition recognizes that managers at all levels of the hierarchy may play a role in strategic renewal and that their behavior may be both purposeful and inadvertent (Mintzberg,

1978). In addition, since most organizations are not divided into sub-units for purposes of capability deployment and capability accumulation, accepting both as interwoven aspects of the renewal process may provide a realistic basis for specifying the administrative mechanisms associated with long-term adaptability.

Indeed, as is evident from our discussion in the introduction, the core processes associated with renewal (idea generation, initiative development, and integration; see Figure I.1), while separable as theoretical constructs, are inherently interdependent. In Chapter 6, we lay out the interdependencies more thoroughly and suggest that the strategic renewal process unfolds much like a complex adaptive system (Waldrop, 1992). This means that strategic change occurs as the outcome of interactions among dozens, hundreds, or even thousands of individuals and groups both within and outside the organization. The change process is so complex that some observers have described it as chaotic (Peters, 1987; Stacey, 1995). Our view is that resource accumulation is socially complex, idiosyncratic, and causally ambiguous (as described by RBV theorists). But the successful adaptation of some organizations suggests that an emergent order can develop out of initial chaos (Kauffman, 1995).

The implication of this line of reasoning, and our third point, is that the evolutionary model is limited in its ability to account for strategic change (White, Marin, Brazeal, & Friedman, 1997). In particular, Burgelman's (1983b, 1983c, 1991, 1994) exclusive reliance on selection within the intraorganizational environment to account for strategic renewal leaves us with an incomplete account of the internal order observed in the renewal process. In fact, for Burgelman (1991), processes that induce a new strategic order (i.e., domain-changing strategic reorientations driven by top managers) are likely to increase the organization's exposure to selection pressures in the external environment. For Burgelman, the constructive role of top management in the strategic renewal processes is limited to its effect on organizational arrangements—that is, the internal selection environment. Thus, by (a) partitioning strategic change into renewal and reorientation processes, (b) describing one as bottom-up and the other as top-down, and (c) relying exclusively on selection as the sole engine of renewal, Burgelman does not consider the full range of interdependencies that characterize strategic change, and he may have underestimated the role of conscious adaptation.

Table 3.2   Motors of Organizational Change

	Prescribed	*Constructive*
Multiple Entities	Evolution	Dialectic
Single Entity	Life Cycle	Teleology

SOURCE: Adapted from Van de Ven and Poole (1995).

Motors of Strategic Renewal

In an astonishingly thorough review of the literature, Van de Ven and Poole (1995) identify four "motors" of organizational change and classify them according to whether they are constructive or prescribed and whether they apply to single or multiple entities (see Table 3.2). Life cycle models portray change as a pattern of development from start-up to growth, maturity, and, ultimately, decline or termination. Such models are prescriptive in the sense that they are linear, irreversible, and inevitable as a fundamental "law of nature." Put differently, this is a change process in which one knows the outcome at the beginning of the process.

The evolutionary change motor is similar in its deterministic character. The difference, however, is that the process is probabilistic, meaning that variety of form at the population level is random and that entities embedded in such a process have no real control over form and adaptation. Another difference, of course, is that evolutionary models apply to populations (i.e., multiple entities). In the case of Burgelman's model of strategic renewal, "entities" refer to autonomous strategic initiatives. Ironically, then, Burgelman's description of autonomous strategic processes is based on a model of change in which order is imposed from the external environment and the behavior of entities is anything but autonomous. Put differently, the prescriptive and probabilistic nature of the evolutionary model leaves little room for the concept of emergent order, the kind of order that emerges from complex and interdependent interactions among people and groups in the process of strategic renewal.

Burgelman (1991, 1994) represents this disorder as a political process. He positions top managers as defenders of the order and keepers of the official strategy. Challenges to current strategy emanate from the external selection environment, but responses are often championed by middle- and operating-level managers. Middle managers especially have an interest in synthesizing reality and controlling the agenda (Dutton & Ashford, 1993; Floyd & Wooldridge, 1992), and, frequently, they have the power to do it (Floyd & Wooldridge, 1997; Hinings, Hickson, Pennings, & Schneck, 1974; Kanter, 1983).

Thus, besides the evolutionary model and the life cycle model, there are two other motors of change (Van de Ven & Poole, 1995). Including these in the concept of strategic renewal provides a more comprehensive and accurate description. Dialectical models of change are driven by the metaphor of opposition or conflict. Change therefore occurs as the result of forces with contradictory interests or values engaging in a recurrent sequence of confrontation, conflict, and synthesis. The dialectical motor typically applies to multiple entities, such as interest groups or coalitions within organizations. It is constructive in the sense that outcomes emerge out of collective action rather than as the result of natural forces or environmental selection.

Finally, and perhaps most familiar in strategic management, teleological change theories emphasize the role of purposeful cooperation. Change is created by the sequence of setting goals, searching for alternative means, implementing goals, and adapting based on the level of satisfaction with perceived outcomes. Teleological theories typically apply to a single entity and are constructive in the sense that goals are socially constructed representations of future states that are envisioned based on past action (Weick, 1995). Moreover, like dialectical theory, this motor is not deterministic. That is, it does not prescribe "which trajectory . . . the organizational entity will follow" (Van de Ven & Poole, 1995, p. 516).

Both dialectical and teleological models appear frequently in the strategy process literature. As noted in Chapter 2, opposition, self-interest, and conflict are the principal features of political models of strategic decision making (Allison, 1971; Braybrooke & Lindblom, 1963; Eisenhardt & Zbaracki, 1992; Narayanan & Fahey, 1982; Quinn, 1980), and reaching consensus on goals and means is equally fundamental in models of strategic planning (Bourgeois, 1985; Lorange & Vancil, 1977; Miller & Cardinal, 1994; Wooldridge & Floyd, 1989). Researchers have even investigated the difference between dialectical inquiry (i.e., induced conflict) and consensus (i.e., agreement on ends and means) as methods of strategy formulation (Schweiger, Sandberg, & Ragan, 1986; Schweiger, Sandberg, & Rechner, 1989). In fact, Burgelman (1983b, 1983c, 1994) recognizes the importance of political skill and strategic intent, but by framing his analysis in purely evolutionary terms, he disconnects political and teleological change processes from strategic renewal. Perhaps Burgelman would recognize this as a limitation of his work, or perhaps he would argue that integrating such diverse theoretical perspectives serves no useful purpose.

From our point of view, however, the weakness of a purely evolutionary conceptualization is an overemphasis on variation as the key factor in strategic renewal. In a purely evolutionary model, there is no chance of strategic renewal unless there is a sufficient variety among strategic initiatives. That is, absent the variety requisite to producing an idea or initiative that will facilitate appropriate organizational change, there is zero probability that adaptation will result. Therefore, autonomy at operating levels, experimentation, and learning become the critical factors in determining renewal outcomes. Although we agree that these are important, the purely evolutionary view overstates the role of chance in successful renewal.

Put differently, variation without order leads to chaos, not a coherent strategy. In an evolutionary model, the primary source of variance reduction is environmental selection. For strategic renewal, this means that order comes from a winnowing process in which certain initiatives are supported while others die out for lack of resources. Selection is not random. Whether an initiative goes on to become a strategic alternative is governed by the structural context that is put into place by top management. This includes administrative mechanisms, such as strategic planning and capital allocation rules, and cultural mechanisms, such as socialization rituals and behavioral norms (Burgelman, 1991). Coherence, then, comes from the "tight coupling between the organizational strategy and strategic initiatives of managers at various levels" provided by the structural context (Burgelman, 1991, p. 244).

Burgelman's description of renewal does not neglect the *fact* that order-inducing processes are necessary in strategic renewal. His clinical description of the process at Intel, for example, acknowledges the importance of top managers' intent and middle managers' political skills. Because his description relies so heavily on evolutionary theory, however, the theoretical account of these processes is incomplete. In particular, we would argue that a more robust description is possible by combining dialectical and teleological theory with the evolutionary approach. This is consistent with Van de Ven and Poole's (1995) recommendation that scholars "identify aspects of motors or relationships that are incompletely described in a given theory" (p. 532).

We believe that an adequate basis for research on strategic renewal from the middle-level perspective combines evolutionary, dialectical, and teleological theory. Specifically, and consistent with Burgelman, we argue that an evolutionary account is needed to explain the relationship between the generation of ideas and strategic renewal. For ideas to become initiatives, however, we will suggest that a dialectical motor takes over in the form of the political processes associated with the formation of coalitions and with the integration of nascent competencies into the organization's established capability base. This is consistent with the general description in Huff et al. (1992), in which the acceptance of change occurs, in part, as a "deal-making" process between various organizational members and groups. In addition, we will identify a teleological motor as the principal driver of change in the official goals and strategy of the organization and in defining the context for new ideas. Incorporating deliberate processes resonates with top-down models of strategic change (e.g., Hamel & Prahalad, 1989). In our description, renewal is a complex adaptive process, however, and this means that order-inducing mechanisms, such as the definition of an organizational goal, are more likely to follow—rather than precede—the emergence of ideas and the generation of strategic alternatives.

The hoped-for benefits of this broader theoretical horizon include a more thorough and robust explanation of the capability development process. Grounding process descriptions in evolutionary, political, and teleological models of change should permit a more detailed description of the relevant phenomena. Dialectical and teleological theory help to further specify internal organizational dynamics and provide richer explanations for each stage of strategic renewal.

One of the challenges of this theoretical approach is to specify the relationships among the three motors of change as they act on the capability development process. This means more than showing how each contributes separately to an explanation of different stages of strategic renewal. To make the model coherent, it must be integrative as well as comprehensive. It must explain how one process connects to or feeds the next, detailing the connections between evolutionary, political, and teleological forces. Unless these connections can be identified, we will be left with theories for three separate processes related to strategic renewal.

Such connections can only be described as microlevel processes (i.e., the interactions between individuals and groups that accompany strategic change). The question then becomes, Where can we observe these interactions? Where in the organization do evolutionary, political, and teleological forces converge?

The Case for a Middle-Level Perspective on Strategic Renewal

Activities that researchers identify as related to strategic change have been found at all levels of the organization—top, middle, and operating levels (Burgelman, 1983c; Floyd & Wooldridge, 1992; Hart, 1992; Johnson & Huff, 1998). To some degree, therefore, investigators may find strategic behavior any place in the organization. That said, it does not follow that all points of observation have the same potential for understanding how firms accumulate critical assets and develop new capabilities.

We have already alerted the reader to our belief that the middle level of the organization is especially important. What is the case for adopting a middle-level perspective? Stated differently, where do researchers stand the best chance of observing the strategic renewal process in a way that informs and complements the top management perspective, which is already established in the literature?

Horizontal Analysis

One way to address these questions might be through a "horizontal analysis." Hrebiniak and Snow (1982), for example, were able to show that certain functional departments were more important than others in defining an organization's distinctive competence. Similarly, Leonard-Barton (1992) noted the connection between core capabilities and dominant disciplines within organizations. Horizontal differentiation of this kind is associated with an organization's attempt to divide work and specialize activity in a way that leads to increased learning and efficiency. Hrebiniak and Snow (1982) reasoned that competitive conditions caused certain types of functional expertise to be more important than others. Porter (1985) makes a similar point in his argument that certain activities in the value chain are likely to be more important to competitive advantage than others. This is consistent with the analysis recommended by Wernerfelt (1984) to identify firm-level critical resources and with empirical research on the role of functional capabilities (e.g., Mascarenhas & Aaker, 1989; Mehra, 1996) in competitive advantage.

Examining the resource configuration of a firm by analyzing its functional competencies is useful when the purpose is to make a link between resources, competitive advantage, and firm-level performance. In fact, research of this kind may be essential to establish the empirical validity of the RBV. Even if the resources associated with advantage tend to be concentrated in horizontally differentiated subunits, however, it does not follow that the processes associated with the accumulation of these resources are defined along functional lines.

More specifically, there are three closely related reasons why a horizontal analysis is not likely to lead to an adequate research strategy for examining the resource accumulation process. First, there is the basic nature of the "process problem." The critical, but neglected, issue is not which resources are related to competitive advantage but *how they came to be accumulated.* Industry conditions are dynamic. Forces such as technology, competitor behavior, and customer needs are constantly reshaping what constitutes a viable competitive advantage. Over the life cycle of a product, for example, different combinations of functional resources may be required to support a competitive position and/or sustain advantage (Hofer, 1975). Thus, the process of developing appropriate resource configurations involves recognizing when conditions demand new resources and responding accordingly. Conceptually, such a process requires a perspective at least one level above that of functionally defined resources in order to incorporate environmental conditions and shifts in functional focus.

Second, although the accumulation process remains largely unspecified, descriptions in the literature consistently suggest that it is an exercise in organizational learning (Burgelman, 1991; Huff et al., 1992; Nelson, 1991; Nelson & Winter, 1982; Teece et al., 1997). Learning at the operational or functional level is important as a means for improving the efficiency with which the organization exploits its existing resource base (Levinthal & March, 1993). Second-order learning of the kind required to accumulate new resources, however, means exploring beyond the boundaries of competence in a given function (Levinthal &

March, 1993). Put differently, the capability to develop new combinations of resources, what Teece et al. (1997) term "dynamic capability," cannot be found within the capability itself (Collis, 1994). Furthermore, because all learning requires an investment of time and attention, there are frequently tradeoffs between the short-term benefits of exploitation and the long-term benefit of investments in exploratory learning. Thus, the resource accumulation process requires a perspective that is sensitive to both short- and long-term priorities.

Third, as Figure 3.2 suggests, the resource accumulation process happens in the context of the organization's current strategic choices (i.e., product scope and resource deployment decisions). Put differently, the decisions and actions associated with the accumulation of future asset stocks are, in part, a function of current flow decisions. The accumulation of technological resources (assets and skills) related to a future product design capability, for example, is partly determined by current decisions to allocate resources for hiring a pool of design engineers. Comprehending the implications of current decisions (e.g., who to hire) for future resource configurations (e.g., product design capabilities), however, requires an understanding of the organization's competitive position and strategic intent. Without such reference points, there is no way to interpret the relative magnitude or character of needed capabilities or to understand the potential resource gap—strategic risk—facing the firm.

In sum, accumulating resources in a way that minimizes strategic risk requires (a) the development of new resources and new combinations of resources, (b) an appropriate investment in both short- and long-term learning, and (c) an understanding of how resource investments are related to current strategy. Each of these challenges involves a process that connects lower-order to higher-order knowledge or tasks. Conceptually, therefore, theory should focus on the activities that link functional resources to resource configurations, short-term priorities to long-term priorities, and accumulation decisions to current strategy.

Vertical Connections in the Resource Accumulation Process

Mintzberg's (1983) configurational theory of organization design helps in defining the vertical connections we are describing and provides more theoretical grounding to the trilobite metaphor. In particular, he differentiates organizations into six subcomponents, including the strategic apex, the middle line, and the operating core. Using this framework, the top management perspective focuses on behavior at the strategic apex, and this is well suited for investigating the formulation of positioning strategy. Behavior in the operating core, on the other hand, represents the knowledge, skills, and capabilities of the organization that are deployed in pursuit of the current strategy and that are employed in learning how to compete better in the future. Connections are made between intended and realized strategy, between the apex and the operating core, in the middle line. Linking activities performed in the middle of the organization include interventions in structure, systems, and staffing that install deliberate strategy as well as those that facilitate the formation of emergent strategy. Also included are processes that reconcile divergent behavior from below with direction from top management.

Wedged between strategy and operations, therefore, the middle line is at the confluence of deliberate, emergent, and realized strategy. It is here that the links between day-to-day decisions (e.g., what kind of engineers to hire), current strategy, and future intent are maintained. Those in the middle are also forced to confront questions about the relationship between functional resources and the configuration needed in the competitive environment. It is the middle line, moreover, that routinely faces the tradeoffs between short- and long-term gains.

In short, our argument is that both theory and research suggest a middle-level perspective as the best opportunity to observe the linking processes associated with learning and the accumulation of resources. Given this, we now turn to the task of outlining the substance of a middle-level perspective. First, in the closing section of this chapter, we identify a set of assumptions specifying the boundaries of this perspective. These are offered as a point of contrast to the assumptions identified in the top management perspective and also to provide a point of departure for developing a substantive statement of the middle-level perspective—a task that occupies the remainder of this book. Then, as a transition to the second part of the book, we provide a conceptual guide to the literature in the area, including established process theories, knowledge, and network models.

An Alternative Set of Assumptions
for Strategy Process Research

Table 3.3 presents three assumptions that we think are necessary for conducting strategy process research in the future and that are particularly important for a middle-level perspective. The first holds that, in continuously changing environments, sustained competitive advantage reflects a firm's dynamic capability (i.e., its ability to renew its capability set). Typically, firms relying on centralized decision making have had trouble responding to continuous change. In many cases, these firms have experienced relatively long periods of stability in which strategic effectiveness, and hence performance, has gradually declined (Johnson, 1987). At some point, a crisis has ensued and radical "frame-breaking" change has been needed to rescue the firm from disaster (Tushman, Newman, & Romanelli, 1986). In contrast, strategic renewal emphasizes continuous adaptation and focuses on learning as an ongoing effort to keep the firm aligned with its environment. This is consistent with Teece et al.'s (1997) theory of competitive advantage and provides the basis of a middle-level perspective.

In contrast to an emphasis on strategic decision making, the second assumption is that renewal results from complex patterns of social interaction. This is a very broad statement, and it is meant to identify the importance of including a variety of organizational actors at various levels and functions within and outside the organization. This radical departure from an "upper-echelons perspective" derives from the resource-based view of strategy. According to the RBV, strategically valuable capabilities combine the skills and knowledge of individuals and groups with the assets and technology of the organization (Barney, 1991). These combinations lead to the development of organizational routines, including learning routines, which are critical to the efficient exploitation of resources and, hence, competitive advantage (Nelson, 1991). In short, the RBV's depiction of competitive advantage suggests that process researchers take a holistic look at the social processes underlying strategic change.

Finally, while recognizing the "field level" of analysis (Scott, 1995) in defining its boundaries, the middle-level perspective focuses attention on the middle of the organization. As we have just argued, the information, knowledge, and social influence most relevant to the development of organizational capabilities are likely to be concentrated in the

Table 3.3 Critical Assumptions for Strategy Process Research and for a
Middle-Level Perspective on Competitive Advantage

1. Sustaining competitive advantage depends on an organization's ability to renew its capabilities by promoting and accommodating new knowledge and innovative behavior.
2. New capabilities emerge from socially complex processes that are embedded in existing knowledge and social relationships.
3. Decisions and actions that occur at middle levels of the organization are at the center of the organizational processes associated with strategic renewal.

middle of the organization. This is the point where critical connections are made between functions and resource configurations, short- and long-term gains, and strategy and operations. The middle line, then, is at the center of strategic renewal.

This third assumption does not mean that the top and operating levels are unimportant or that they have no role in strategic renewal. Indeed, they merit study in their own right. We do assert, however, that because the knowledge and activities associated with renewal are most prevalent in the middle line, process researchers (especially those interested in dynamic environments) stand to gain the most by focusing their attention at this level. This chapter has presented a limited amount of evidence for this assertion. In reality, we are like prospectors who assume that there is valuable insight to be found where we are pointing. The purpose of this book is to convince others to join the search.

Relevant Literature and Conclusions

Figure 3.3 offers a guide to how the literature reviewed in the book addresses these shifts. As the figure shows, Part I of the book has been dedicated to setting the context. We reviewed foundational process literature, described its limitations in explaining capability development, and argued that a middle-level perspective is needed to fill the gap. This new perspective creates two shifts in the focus of strategy process research. First, it reconceives strategy not as a decision-making activity but as a social learning process. Second, it shifts attention away from top managers and toward individuals and groups located in the middle of the organization.

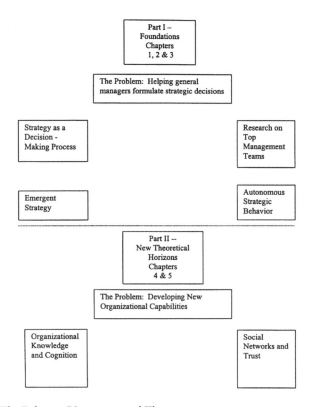

Figure 3.3. The Relevant Literatures and Theory

We focus on the first of these shifts in Part II. Two issues appear critical in reconceiving strategy as a social learning process: Where does the impetus for learning come from, and how does such learning spread throughout the organization? The question of how organizations learn points us to the topic of organizational knowledge. We have already suggested the generation of new ideas as the theoretical starting point for strategic renewal. Where such ideas come from and how they develop into action are the main concern of the literatures on organizational knowledge and managerial cognition. Although these two areas of inquiry have appeared relatively recently in the organizational sciences, they have deep routes in philosophy and psychology. Thus, in Chapter 4, we review both epistemological and cognitive explanations for knowledge development and define certain key concepts and relationships to be used in Chapter 6.

Chapter 5 is concerned not with knowledge itself but with how it is diffused within the organization. In this regard, the theory and research associated with social networks offer a very useful connection between information transfer and influence processes. More than just a set of empirical techniques, social network theory represents a set of core concepts that account for the emergence of novel information and new patterns of interaction among organization members. Still, social relationships are more than exchanges of information. To complete our description of socializing, we therefore turn to the literature on politics and organizational trust. By combining notions of self-interest and conflict with those of reciprocity and cooperation, Chapter 5 offers up a rich foundation for characterizing the complexity of human relationships.

As we have already acknowledged, our theory development process was iterative. That is, although we set out to focus only on knowledge and social networks, after working on the model, we found that we needed a deeper appreciation for politics and trust. Thus, although we have tried to be careful about defining the scope of our review and drawing attention to particular ideas, readers should be aware that neither Chapter 4 nor 5 is exhaustive. But any good review has an agenda. Ours is twofold: reconceptualizing the core constructs in strategy process research and creating a theoretical foundation for a middle-level perspective. Part III is dedicated to the second part of our agenda.

Notes

1. In reality, of course, the top management perspective is not a theory but a collection of theories that have a set of assumptions in common.

2. More detail on the kind of research we have in mind is provided in Chapters 6 and 7.

3. Information about the trilobite comes from the University of California Museum of Paleontology Web site, *www.ucmp.berkeley.edu.*

4. At this writing, a few texts have moved away from the dichotomy (e.g., Barney, 1996; Collis & Montgomery, 1997). Still, a review of leading texts and syllabi from more than 30 prominent business schools performed by the authors in 1995 and 1994, respectively, shows that the distinction continues to be fundamental to how strategic management is taught. For example, the restructuring of the curriculum at Harvard Business School in 1996 continued the tradition with separate MBA strategy courses in formulation and implementation.

5. For purposes of a consistent syntax, it may be useful to distinguish between resource allocation—a decision process that assumes that a given resource is fungible, and hence allocable, to numerous uses (e.g., resources such as financial capital, people, information)—and resource de-

ployment, which assumes that resources are heterogeneous by nature (e.g., firm-specific assets and skills) and hence deployable only in specific contexts.

6. Obvious examples of top management accumulation, such as mergers and acquisitions, are not necessarily where they play their greatest role. Indeed, integrating the knowledge from an acquisition often falls to middle management. More interesting examples of top management accumulation include their use of informal influence in political channels or with regulatory authorities.

II

New Theoretical Horizons: Organizational Knowledge, Social Networks, and Trust

4 Organizational Knowledge and Strategic Renewal

> It is the middle manager that . . . combines strategic, macro, universal information and hands-on, micro, specific information. They work as a bridge between the visionary ideals of the top and the often chaotic reality of the frontline of business. (Nonaka, 1994, p. 32)

Recent work on organizational knowledge ranges from descriptions of organizational memory (Walsh & Ungson, 1991), to techniques for mapping managers' mental models (Barr, Stimpert, & Huff, 1992; Calori, Johnson, & Sarnin, 1994), to studies of knowledge transfer within (Szulanski, 1996) and between organizations (Lane & Lubatkin, 1998). The theoretical and methodological traditions of these research streams are often quite separate, and the ideas of one may not inform the other (Huber, 1991). In many cases, scholars may not even use the word *knowledge* to describe the central construct, choosing instead words such as *meaning, sense making, learning, cognition,* or *intelligence.* This situation makes a comprehensive review of the literature impractical.

Our interest in organizational knowledge, however, is motivated by the need to explain managerial behavior at the middle level and to describe the processes associated with the development and deployment of organizational capability. Strategic renewal is a social learning process, and we must therefore concern ourselves with what organizational knowledge is and how it develops. This directs us to four pairs of closely related questions that guide and constrain the discussion.

- What is organizational knowledge, and what are the criteria used to differentiate true knowledge from falsehood in organizations?
- How do organizations assimilate and accept new ideas, and how do they create new organizational knowledge?
- What is the locus of organizational knowledge, and how is it transferred, integrated, and coordinated?
- When is knowledge a critical resource, and what is the relationship between organizational knowledge and competitive advantage?

We use these questions to organize a review of existing work and to show how it relates to the middle-level perspective. With epistemology as background, we summarize in Table 4.1 the way writers describe the assimilation of new ideas and the creation of knowledge in organizations. Then we focus on the locus of organizational knowledge. Identifying pockets of knowledge in organizations is important since we are calling for a shift in where researchers should look for it. Once we understand what knowledge is and where it comes from, the key issue is how to transfer, combine, and coordinate it within an organization. Finally, at the end of the chapter, we return to the reason for our interest in knowledge: its role in strategic renewal and competitive advantage.

What Is Organizational Knowledge?

The nature of organizational knowledge may be one of the most complex and controversial issues facing management researchers. Most scholars in the area would agree that knowledge is "created and organized by the . . . flow of information" (Nonaka, 1994, p. 15), but otherwise there is great diversity in the literature. Two broad distinctions frame the discussion: objective versus subjective knowledge criteria and tacit versus explicit types of knowledge.

Objective and Subjective Acceptance of Ideas

Organizational knowledge is embedded in technologies, routines, social structures, norms, and shared values (Nelson & Winter, 1982;

Walsh & Ungson, 1991). Therefore, the knowledge of individuals—even in the aggregate—is not equivalent to organizational knowledge. For an individual's idea to become part of organizational knowledge (i.e., a technology, routine, etc.), it must be accepted and acted on by other members. Acceptance involves testing and dialogue, and, as we show later, middle-level actors are central to the process.

In the process of acceptance, ideas are likely to face both objective and subjective criteria (Spender, 1996; Weick, 1995). Objective criteria are based on the notion that what we know is a function of what exists—that is, empirical reality. Subjective criteria are based on the notion that what exists is a function of what we know—that is, that we enact our reality (Daft & Weick, 1984). Thus, an idea for a new product may be considered objectively against a background of empirical market research. Whether the product is actually developed, however, may also depend on top management's subjective interpretation of these "realities."

As a part of strategic renewal, it may seem more important to take an objective approach to the acceptance of ideas. After all, producing good financial outcomes appears to depend on recognizing and responding to independent economic realities (competitors, customers, regulators, etc.). On the other hand, renewal also demands new ideas and innovative behavior. These develop from the subjective, idiosyncratic insight of individuals and the willingness of others to adopt empirically unexamined and objectively risky beliefs. Subjective criteria in the form of firm culture (Barney, 1992) and strategic intent (Hamel & Prahalad, 1989) have thus been suggested as stimulants for creativity and renewal (Kogut & Zander, 1992; Nonaka, 1994). In organizations that are successful over the long haul, the process of acceptance—the development of knowledge—likely depends on both objective and subjective knowledge criteria.

Tacit and Explicit Knowledge

A related distinction in the knowledge literature is the difference between knowledge that can be articulated and knowledge that cannot be articulated but that is still known in some sense. Polanyi (1967) formulated this as the difference between explicit and tacit knowledge. For example, scientific creativity begins with the subjective, tacit intuition of a researcher who, immersed in his or her subject, is flooded with subconscious insight. The scientific process proceeds, then, by making this highly subjective, inarticulable "hunch" explicit, testing it against empirical observation, and sharing the result with the community.

According to Spender (1996), Nelson and Winter (1982) were the first to introduce the *explicit/tacit* terminology into the organizational literature. For them, knowledge is embodied as a set of "routines," some of which are explicit (e.g., rules, procedures, etc.) and some of which are tacit (e.g., cultural norms). Spender (1996) himself uses the terms *explicit* and *implicit* to characterize the distinction and describes the latter as incorporating subconscious or preconscious forms of knowledge.

Tacit knowledge is important in strategy because it is difficult—if not impossible—to imitate. Thus, although a firm may be able to replicate the scientific technology associated with a rival's product, it will not be able to duplicate the culture and routines of the organization. As a result, transferring technology may not result in the transfer of organizational capability. Put differently, when tacit knowledge forms the foundation of core capability, it erects a barrier to imitation by rivals.

The notion of tacitness complicates the question of what constitutes knowledge because it suggests that we know more than we consciously believe. This difficulty goes away, however, if one recognizes action over articulation as the measure of belief. Assuming that knowledge in one form or another causes human behavior, then one can tell what is known by observing actions as well as assertions. Indeed, this is a premise of most philosophy and common sense. It may not be possible for skilled cyclists to articulate what they know about riding, but their beliefs about technique can be observed directly from their behavior.

Definitions and Sources of Knowledge

Table 4.1 identifies definitions of organizational knowledge, sources of knowledge, and the distinctions underlying key constructs in the organizational literature. (See Grant, 1996; Huber, 1991; Kogut & Zander, 1992; Spender, 1996; Walsh & Ungson, 1991, for more complete reviews of the literature.)

As Table 4.1 suggests, there are a number of perspectives on knowledge. We do not have space to review each of these but, instead, have chosen to focus on managerial cognition, sense making, and shared belief as the basis for the model described in Chapter 6. The purpose of

Table 4.1 Constructs Related to Organizational Knowledge: Definitions, Sources, and Distinctions

	Definition of Organizational Knowledge	*Sources of Organizational Knowledge*	*Acceptance Criteria and Knowledge Type*	*Representative Citations*
Economics	Decision-making capacity	Rationality, data, information	Objective and explicit	Simon (1947)
	Coherent action	Routines	Empirical and tacit	Nelson and Winter (1982)
	Shared belief	Individuals, managers, entrepreneurs	Subjective and tacit	Nonaka (1994)
Sociology	Rules, tasks, technology	Structure, roles, physical surroundings	Objective and explicit	Durkheim (1933)
	Assumptions, culture	Artifacts, rituals, norms, values	Empirical and tacit	Schein (1985)
	Sense making, shared meaning, ideology	Identity, interpretation, language, symbols, culture	Subjective and tacit	Burrell and Morgan (1979)
Psychology	Intelligence	Data, information	Objective and explicit	Simon (1947)
	Learning	Experience, search	Empirical and tacit	Argyris and Schon (1978)
	Cognition	Consciousness, unconscious (tacit) or subconscious, beliefs, perceptions, scripts and schemas	Subjective and tacit	Kiesler and Sproull (1982)

the table is simply to provide a broader grounding for our definition of *organizational knowledge* and to call the reader's attention to the wider literature.

The definition of *organizational knowledge* used in this book is tailored to its focus on strategic renewal, on how organizations "learn to do new things" (Nelson, 1991). Thus, *organizational knowledge is accu-*

mulated as individual members encounter information, interpret it, and interact with one another in the process of pursuing their collective interests. What individuals in organizations believe to be known is based on the information that is available to them in the form of prior beliefs (conscious or subconscious), objective data, (boundedly) rational thinking, and, importantly, ideas communicated in the words and deeds of others. What organizations know can be judged by examining the collective behavior of their members and by the social structures, symbols, and artifacts used to govern organized activity. Thus, in the development of capability, organizational knowledge is a function of what members believe and how this belief is translated into organizational action.

What Is the Locus of Organizational Knowledge? How Is Knowledge Created, Transferred, and Integrated?

Since 1990, a considerable amount of work has been done to locate organizational knowledge, to explain where it comes from and how it is applied. Actually, two literature streams, managerial cognition and organizational knowledge, have emerged within strategic management.

Work on managerial cognition has benefited from a well-developed research methodology in psychology. A number of rigorous studies have examined relationships between managers' mental maps and various constructs from strategic management theory (e.g., Calori et al., 1994; Reger & Huff, 1993). Work on organizational knowledge has been somewhat more theoretical, and empirical methods remain underdeveloped, often relying on anecdotes and questionnaires, for example. Still, much progress has been made in both arenas.

Managerial Cognition

This approach assumes that organizational action can be understood by examining the mental models of influential managers (Barr et al., 1992; Huff, 1990; Kiesler & Sproull, 1982). Mental models are the set of concepts and relationships through which an individual comprehends the world around him or her (Weick & Bougon, 1986). Given humans' limited ability to process information, these "maps" or "schema" simplify the virtually infinite set of data presented in organizational settings. This allows decision makers to discern overall patterns and perceive the "big picture" (e.g., the strategy) in the situation (Huff, 1990).

There is always the danger that such perceptual filters will be "inaccurate" or false in a positivistic sense. Quoting Korzybski, Weick (1990) notes, "The map is not the territory" (p. 2). The world simply may not be the way we think it is. Nonetheless, the way influential managers think about their strategic "space"—such as who their competitors are and how their rivals' strategies differ from one another—is closely associated with firm behavior (Reger & Huff, 1993). Indeed, the "accuracy" of managers' mental maps may not be important in understanding their behavior. Consider the famous Hungarian detachment who "found their way" out of the Alps with a map of the Pyrenees (Holub, 1977, as cited in Weick, 1995, p. 4).

"Sense making" (Starbuck & Milliken, 1988; Weick, 1995; Westley, 1990) provides a rich description of the processes that lead to the creation of individual and organizational cognitive frameworks. Sense making "literally . . . means the making of sense" (Weick, 1995, p. 4). The notion is that people respond to the world around them by constructing mental frameworks within which the various cues and stimuli can be organized and understood. People need a frame of reference before they can "comprehend, understand, explain, attribute, extrapolate and predict" (Starbuck & Milliken, 1988, p. 51). It is important to recognize that sense making is more than an interpretation of reality based on a conceptual schema. Sense making includes the creation of the schema itself. As Weick (1995) states, sense making is "about authoring as well as reading" (p. 7); it is about "creation as well as discovery" (p. 8). Knowledge is constructed by organizing sensory perceptions within a conceptual framework, and the truth of beliefs is judged by their consistency with the framework. Sense making is about the construction of knowledge.

Weick (1995) identifies seven properties of sense making—four of which we review here—that provide a shorthand approach for describing the theory.[1] First, sense making is grounded in the construction of identity. That is, people understand the world around them based on their self-concepts. Notice that the word *self-concepts* is plural because the process is ongoing and occurs in multiple contexts, including families, love relationships, and organizations (Dutton & Dukerich, 1991). Second, sense making is retrospective because reality is always in the past, or at least our perception of reality is. "We are conscious always of what we have done, never of doing it" (Mead, 1956, as cited in Weick, 1995, p. 26). The retrospective character of sense making is important because it signals the fact that the frameworks people create are built on past events and then used to understand later circumstances. With the passage of time, hindsight often tends to impose order and tighten causal connections between events. Third, sense making is enactive of sensible environments. The situation people face (i.e., the stimuli in the environment) is really closely connected to their behavior. "Sensemaking keeps action and cognition together" (Weick, 1995, p. 31). Ordinary people are very much like legislators in this way; they take an otherwise undifferentiated environment and define categories, boundaries, and so on by thinking about it (Weick, 1995). As noted earlier, for Weick, enactment does not mean that there is no objective reality. It simply means that people define the reality around them based on what they are doing at the time. Finally, sense making is social. What goes on inside our heads and how we behave is defined by how others behave toward us. Much of social interaction is in the form of discourse, and therefore language itself is a very important element of the mental model. Language provides the structure. Language is what "brackets reality" (Weick, 1995).

Empirical research in this vein has focused on a number of topics related to the strategy process, including policy making (Feldman, 1989), socialization processes (Louis, 1980), strategic decision making (Gioia & Chittipeddi, 1991; Westley, 1990), strategic issue management (Dutton & Ottensmeyer, 1987), industry recipes (Spender, 1989), CEOs' perceptions (Fiol, 1989), and corporate renewal (Hurst, Rush, & White, 1989). Typically, the methods employed by these studies involve interviews, field observations, case studies, and grounded theory. This is because sense-making research is about describing the sense people are making of a situation. By overstructuring the observation process, researchers could easily fall prey to *imposing their own sense* on the data.

In contrast, much of the other empirical literature on managerial cognition uses a highly structured mapping process. Often, the purpose is to capture the cause-effect relationships, or "cause maps," held by managers about events around them (Huff, 1990).[2] Huff (1990) defines five types of maps or mapping processes: maps that assess attention, association, and importance; maps that show dimensions of categories and cognitive taxonomies; maps that show influence, causality, and system dynamics; maps that show the structure of argument and conclusion; and maps that specify schemas, frames, and perceptual codes. Although maps may oversimplify the sense-making process, Huff (1990, pp. 6-8) argues that this simplicity is appropriate for strategic management cognition studies because "getting the big picture" is precisely the point.

A key theme in this research is the role of mental models in organizational change, and this is why managerial cognition is relevant to strategic renewal. Researchers have found that mental models affect what individuals notice in the environment (Kiesler & Sproull, 1982; Nisbett & Ross, 1980). For example, an organization may be facing a problem that threatens its survival, but relevant facts may go unnoticed by managers if the data do not fit the managers' mental models (Whetten, 1988). Moreover, even if relevant facts are noticed, existing schema affect the interpretation given to environmental stimuli. In the process, objective threats may be discounted, and this prevents the organization from acting in the absence of a real crisis.

Thus, the need for changes in organization behavior that may be apparent to others may not be seen by those who are responsible for strategic decisions (Dutton & Jackson, 1987; Sapienza, 1987). When managers do spot negative signals, the tendency is to attribute poor results to external factors "beyond their control" (Huff, 1990; Huff, Huff, & Thomas, 1992; Staw, McKechnie, & Puffer, 1993). In the context of strategic renewal, it is therefore important to encourage strategic thinking and to foster divergent ideas throughout the organization.

Creating Organizational Knowledge and the Knowledge-Based Theory of the Firm

Theorists who have aligned themselves with the concept of organizational knowledge rather than managerial cognition tend to take a "macro" or sociological approach. They treat knowledge more as "how people socialize" than as "what people think," and this puts a greater emphasis on social interaction as the locus and theoretical focal point of knowledge. Moreover, whereas cognitionists concern themselves with mapping knowledge that already exists, researchers in the organizational knowledge domain are more concerned about where knowledge comes from and how it moves around in the organization. In this regard, some of what has been written is notable for its bearing on a middle-level perspective.

For example, Ikujiro Nonaka puts middle managers at the center of his discussion of organizational innovation and knowledge creation (Nonaka, 1988, 1991, 1994).

> The most important knowledge creating individuals in this model are nei-ther charismatic top managers nor the entrepreneur-like lower managers, but every employee who works in association with middle managers. It is the middle manager that takes a strategic position at which he or she com-bines strategic, macro, universal information and hands-on, micro, specific information. They work as a bridge between the visionary ideals of the top and the often chaotic reality of the frontline of business. . . . Middle manag-ers mediate between "what is" and "what ought to be." (Nonaka, 1994, p. 32)

Underlying Nonaka's emphasis on middle management is his theory of how organizational knowledge is created. Recognizing that the spark of an idea comes from individual intuition, he argues that organiza-tions are important parts of the context in which such sparks occur. Equally important, organizations are the means by which individual ideas are "amplified" and "crystallized" to become part of a broader knowledge network. Within such networks, social interactions at vari-ous levels (i.e., dyads, groups, intraorganizational, interorgani-zational) create knowledge in several different "modes."

Here, Nonaka takes us back to Polanyi's distinction between tacit and explicit knowledge. He believes that explicit knowledge has to be trans-formed into tacit knowledge and vice versa before organizational learning can occur. Specifically, he posits a dynamic spiral of organiza-tional knowledge creation: from explicit to explicit (combination), tacit to tacit (socialization), tacit to explicit (externalization), and ex-plicit to tacit (internalization). These transitions occur as the result of social interactions that are triggered by the need to coordinate behav-ior, dialogue about past experiences, and so forth.

For social constructionists, the "field" within which such interac-tions occur is all important, and Nonaka argues that self-organizing teams are essential building blocks of knowledge within organizations. Self-organization induces the trust necessary for members to share a creative dialogue in which tacit knowledge can be transferred. In addi-tion, the boundaries of self-organized teams are fluid, and this facilitates a variety in perspectives that is consistent with creativity. Finally, it is middle managers who serve as leaders of self-organizing teams, and it is in this role that they mediate between the "vertical and horizontal flows of information in the company" (Nonaka, 1994, p. 32).

It is interesting to note that, although Grant's (1996) knowledge-based theory of the firm is based on the idea that knowledge creation is an individual-level, not an organizational-level, process, the implications of his theory for the bureaucratic model of decision making are strikingly similar to Nonaka's. Grant's premise is that firms exist largely as institutions for applying the specialized knowledge of individuals. This starting point is no different from a transactions cost theory of the firm (Coase, 1937; Williamson, 1975). But, rather than focusing on an analysis of alternative governance mechanisms, Grant focuses on coordination within the firm and the processes of knowledge integration itself. After evaluating numerous coordination mechanisms and the role of organization structure in coordination, Grant observes, "If the primary productive resource of the firm is knowledge, and if knowledge resides in individual employees, then it is employees who own the bulk of the firm's resources" (p. 119). Moreover, because explicit knowledge is difficult to aggregate and tacit knowledge is difficult to transfer, control over strategic decision making must be substantially decentralized.

Nonaka's and Grant's arguments run counter to the assumptions implicit in some of the work in strategy on managerial cognition—that is, that organization knowledge is located in the minds of "influential" (e.g., top) managers.[3] Indeed, most research on organization knowledge recognizes that knowledge is embedded in ongoing activities, or organizational "routines" (Barney, 1991; Conner, 1991; Nelson & Winter, 1982). In addition to the written standard operating procedures one thinks of as routines, many routines represent tacit, taken-for-granted habits depicting the "way things are done around here." Furthermore, in describing organization memory, Walsh and Ungson (1991) identify five different types of retention facilities: individuals, culture, transformations, structures, and ecology. Thus, organizational knowledge is a much broader construct than anticipated in many mapping studies.

In summary, it is important to understand what CEOs are thinking. But it is also important to understand how this thinking is affected by organizational routines, organizational memory, and the beliefs of middle-level managers and others in the organization. Because knowl-

Table 4.2 Similarities and Distinctions Between Managerial Cognition and
Organizational Knowledge

With Regard To	Managerial Cognition	Organizational Knowledge
What is the locus of organizational knowledge?	Minds and behavior of influential individuals	Individuals
		Operating and learning routines
	Organizational memory	Organizational memory
How is knowledge created?	Schema formation, use, and adaptation	Individual intuition
	Action taking	Action taking
	Common experience	Combination
		Socialization
		Externalization
		Internalization
How is knowledge transferred?	Social interaction	Social interaction
	Language	Language
	Communication	Codified communication
	Symbols and artifacts	
How is knowledge integrated?	Collective interpretations	Coordination
	Common ideologies	

edge is scattered throughout the organization, transferring it, moving it from one part of the organization to another, has been a central focus. Researchers have studied knowledge transfer between organizational levels (Floyd & Wooldridge, 1999), between functional departments (Clark & Fujimoto, 1991), between activities within a project (Takeuchi & Nonaka, 1986), between the headquarters and subsidiary organization of a multinational (Kogut & Zander, 1993), and across firms in a joint venture (Lane & Lubatkin, 1998).

Two major themes come through. The first is that, to acquire new knowledge, an organization needs to have a certain level of prior knowledge within a relevant domain (Cohen & Levinthal, 1990). The second point is that the transfer of tacit knowledge is far more problematic than the transfer of explicit knowledge (Subramaniam & Venkatraman, 1998). The latter is more codifiable, more observable, and less complex (Kogut & Zander, 1995) and, therefore, easier to communicate in unambiguous formal language systems. Tacit knowledge, on the other hand, can be acquired only through direct experience (Nonaka & Takeuchi, 1995)—learning by doing. In addition, internalizing tacit knowledge requires rich information processing mechanisms (Daft & Lengel, 1986), such as sense making (Weick, 1995) within cross-functional teams (Nonaka, 1994).

In short, knowledge does appear to be an omnipresent phenomenon within organizations. This is not surprising since organizations consist of people. Though it is everywhere, the right knowledge is often not where we want it when we want it there, and specialized knowledge is often not useful on its own. Thus, the questions of how to create, transfer, and integrate organizational knowledge has preoccupied research to date. Table 4.2 summarizes how the managerial cognition and organizational knowledge literatures address these questions. As the table shows, these literatures have much in common, and where they differ, the differences appear to be complementary, rather than exclusionary.

How Is Organizational Knowledge Related to Other Resources in the Growth of Capability?

Because strategic management is concerned with the economic performance of firms, perhaps the most central issue in a discussion of organizational knowledge is how it helps to explain competitive advantage. There are at least two ways to approach this. One is to see knowledge as a firm resource that, like other resources, may distinguish the firm from its competitors and generate economic rents. In this view, a knowledge-based view of strategy is subsumed under the more general resource-based theory of the firm. A second approach—what might be called the knowledge-based view—operates under the assumption that the knowledgeable behavior of people accounts for all organizational activity, including those instances in which activities produce competitive advantage. Thus, knowledge is not just a potentially advantageous resource; rather, it is the principal force in organizing and provides the basis for an alternative theory of the firm.

Given the disciplinary heritages of these two views (economics and social psychology), it is not surprising that they cut along a key epistemological fault line. The resource-based view (RBV) is grounded solidly in the empirical traditions of modern economics and in its accompanying realist ontology. The cognitive or knowledge-based view superimposes human thought and interpretation onto objective phenomena, such as resources. Knowledge from the objective world is thereby supplanted or supplemented by socially constructed knowledge.

The Resource-Based View of Knowledge

The RBV asserts that firms are different from one another because they possess unique sets of resources, consisting of tangible or intangible assets and capabilities. Examples of resources include brands, patents, cash, individual skills, and knowledge (Grant, 1991). The strategy of the firm is constrained by the resources it controls and by the rate at which it can accumulate new ones (Nelson, 1991). Without resource differences among firms, all firms would be motivated to adopt whatever strategy appeared most successful at any particular moment, and no firm would be able to establish a differentiated competitive position. Hence, controlling the right set of resource stocks at the right time is the essence of achieving competitive advantage.

Barney (1991) has defined the criteria for "the right set of resources": They should be valued in the market, rare, difficult to imitate, nontradable, and nonsubstitutable. As we noted in Chapter 3, however, the theory is less clear about how firms come to possess the resources that meet these criteria. Idiosyncratic firm history (Dierickx & Cool, 1989) and luck (Barney, 1986) play important roles. But managers (Penrose, 1959) and their strategic intentions (Hamel & Prahalad, 1989; Prahalad & Bettis, 1986) are also important. They bring focus and discipline to the accumulation process. They deliberately try to create advantage and encourage the development of some resources more than others (Wernerfelt, 1984).

Economic rents result from valuable factors whose supply is inherently limited. Imperfections in the markets for these factors create a serendipitous, but powerful, advantage for particular firms (Barney, 1986). Actually, this kind of durable advantage may be relatively rare, however (Collis & Montgomery, 1997). More likely, firms possess unique and valuable resources as the result of internal innovation (Conner, 1991). The rents generated from such resources, however, endure only as long as it takes for the innovation to spread to other firms.

Knowledge is incorporated into the RBV as an intangible asset. For example, a firm's unique product design or its marketing capability is a function of the design and marketing expertise of its employees.[4] Thus, one can usefully distinguish knowledge-based resources such as these from property-based resources such as brand names (Miller & Shamsie, 1996).

In the RBV, however, knowledge itself is not the key distinguishing feature of business organizations. It is also not the primary source of competitive advantage. Instead, knowledge is one of many possible sources of competitive advantage, and its importance for the firm depends on context. As Nonaka and Takeuchi (1995) and others argue, however, knowledge may have become the most important strategic factor in many markets. In particular, as a source of Schumpeterian rents, knowledge may be crucial in those industries in which product and process innovation is the basis of competitive advantage (Hayes & Pisano, 1994). Still, in the RBV, knowledge is important only as a function of its value as a resource.

The Knowledge-Based View of Competitive Advantage

The knowledge-based view of competitive advantage starts from a different premise. Rather than seeing firms as bundles of assets, skills, and resources, firms are considered first and foremost as social organizations consisting of individuals who interact with one another on the basis of individual beliefs, shared ideology, or shared interpretations. Walsh and Ungson (1991), for example, define an organization as "a network of inter-subjectively shared meanings that are sustained through the development and use of a common language and everyday social interaction" (p. 60). Similarly, knowledge-based researchers (e.g., Grant, 1996; Kogut & Zander, 1992; Nonaka, 1994; Spender, 1996) propose an alternative theory of the firm based on the efficiencies enjoyed in the creation (Nonaka, 1994), transfer (Kogut & Zander, 1992), or integration (Conner & Prahalad, 1996; Grant, 1996) of knowledge. Nonaka (1994), for example, focuses on how individual knowledge is amplified and applied within the organization.

The literatures on managerial cognition and organizational knowledge share a common emphasis on beliefs, thought processes, knowledge, and interpretations as determinants of firm behavior. To understand what gives organizations unique characteristics such as competitive advantage, according to both these views, one must go be-yond references to objective phenomena such as resources and enter the realm of subjective reality. Whether a firm's strategy is adaptive and whether it enjoys competitive advantage are therefore likely to be a function of how the firm's managers frame and enact the situation fac-ing them (Smircich & Stubbart, 1985). It is important to note, however, that it is actions that are essential in the enactment process, not the "conceptual pictures" they carry around in their heads (Weick, 1995). Put differently, what managers do is what creates the objective reality they face. Thus, from a managerial cognition perspective, the *unique-ness* of managers' mental maps (in comparison to managers in rival firms) may be as important to competitive advantage as their accuracy (in comparison to objective reality; Huff, 1990).

Furthermore, knowledge theorists argue that all human experience is essentially social: What goes on in the minds of individuals cannot be separated from its social context. As Weick (1995) puts it, "What a per-son does internally is contingent on others" (p. 40). In short, whether they describe it in psychological or sociological terms, theorists in this domain hold the view that all decisions and actions within the firm are governed by knowledge. A corollary of this view is that competitive ad-vantage depends on the knowledge embedded within the firm.

Thus, firms are differentiated by the decisions and actions of people within them (Mintzberg, 1978), and these decisions and actions are the result of mental activity that draws on individual or organizational knowledge (Huff, 1990). This is true whether one is focused on a deci-sion maker at the top of the organization or an everyday activity at the operating level (Johnson & Huff, 1998). It is also true whether the ac-tion responds to routine cues or to unexpected events. It applies whether the knowledge is explicit, individual knowledge of the form that might govern the behavior of an individual assembly-line worker or whether the knowledge is tacit, group knowledge of the form that defines organizational culture (Spender, 1996). Moreover, resources under the firm's control are unlikely to add value or to produce com-petitive advantage unless they are leveraged intelligently by managers within the firm (Penrose, 1959). Finally, even when an individual or or-ganization *lacks* the knowledge needed to respond effectively, learning itself draws on knowledge about related subject matter (Cohen & Levinthal, 1990), about the problem-solving process (Levinthal & March, 1993), and about learning how to learn (Argyris & Schon, 1978; Teece, Pisano, & Shuen, 1997).

Knowledge, Capability, and Competitive Advantage

Notice that these assertions lead us to the position that firms can hold no competitive advantage unless it relies somehow on unique knowledge. Rather than a resource-based view of competitive advantage, this view leads to a capability-based view of competitive advantage. Knowledge is what transforms factors into unique and valuable resources within the firm. The firm may control unique assets, but this control itself depends on the knowledge needed to accumulate and deploy such assets. Put differently, the resources underlying competitive advantage are either directly or indirectly capability-based. The resource itself may be a capability, such as Walt Disney's unique ability to entertain people in outdoor settings. But if the resource is an asset, knowledge is required to nurture, deploy, and sustain it as an advantage. Otherwise, the value of an asset can erode. The value of one of Disney's animated figures, for example, could decline as the result of poor licensing decisions.

Collis (1994) argues that such a view falsely portrays organizational capabilities as the "holy grail" of competitive advantage and thereby sends researchers off on a never-ending search for the ultimate capability (p. 144). In large part, his skepticism about the centrality of capability comes out of his observation that, for any capability, a higher-order capability can always be defined. For example, he argues that Disney's ability to entertain people in outdoor settings is really the result of the organizational structures and behaviors that the company has put into place. Hence, it is the capability to develop these structures that is the real capability underlying Disney's advantage. Furthermore, a more valuable capability would be the ability to develop new organizational structures and behaviors that would lead to the development of new capabilities, such as the ability to entertain people in a theatrical setting. But then an even more valuable capability would be the ability to develop the ability to learn how to develop new organizational structures and behaviors of all different kinds that would lead to the development of even better capabilities—that is, the ability to learn how to learn.

The pursuit of competitive advantage leads to an infinite regress until competition occurs over the nth order derivative of the rate of change of position, where no sustainable competitive advantage accrues to anyone because all competitors can almost instantaneously and costlessly match any valuable product market position. (Collis, 1994, p. 144)

Collis (1994) makes an interesting and lively case for the position that some capabilities provide no sustainable advantage because they are either eroded as the firm adapts to change, replaced by a different capability, or, as indicated above, surpassed by a better capability (p. 147). As he acknowledges, however, his view that capabilities are "just another level in the explanation of sustainable competitive advantage with no greater claim to precedence than any other level" (p. 151) is not consistent with other literature on competitive advantage (e.g., Amit & Schoemaker, 1993; Barney, 1992; Lippman & Rumelt, 1982; Stalk, Evans, & Shulman, 1992; Teece et al., 1997). In some measure, this inconsistency is caused by the realist ontology inherent in Collis's purely economic view of knowledge. As long as knowledge and capabilities are seen as purely objective phenomena, they remain on a par with other kinds of resources. This leads to a search for higher-order capabilities to set one resource apart from another, rather than recognizing that knowledge is a qualitatively different kind of resource.

From a subjectivist or social constructionist point of view, however, the knowledge embedded within capabilities develops in the minds and social interactions within the firm. This knowledge is inherently unique because it is grounded in a set of idiosyncratic, subjective experiences. Moreover, subjective perceptions and interpretations, whether at the individual or group level of analysis, are more likely to be tacit, and hence more difficult to imitate (Jain, 1989; Kogut & Zander, 1993; Subramaniam & Venkatraman, 1998; Zander & Kogut, 1995). To paraphrase R. D. Laing, an organization can experience the behavior of another organization (e.g., competitive interactions) and an organization can even experience another organization's experience of it (e.g., by a game-theoretic analysis of its responses), but an organization can never experience another organization's experience.

Indeed, the central role of subjective knowledge and path-dependent experience in competitive advantage is compatible with the notion of dynamic capability (Nelson, 1991; Teece et al., 1997). In this case, the word *dynamic* refers to how a firm "renews competencies so as to achieve congruence with the changing business environment," and *ca-*

Table 4.3   Distinctions Between the Resource-Based and Capability-Based View of Competitive Advantage

	Underlying Premise of the Firm	*Key to Competitive Advantage*	*Role of Knowledge*	*Acceptance Criteria*
Resource-Based View	Firms are different because they possess unique sets of resources.	Valuable, rare, inimitable, and nonsubstitutable resources	One of many possible resources that may or may not be linked to advantage depending on the context	Objectivism
Capability-Based View	Firms are social entities consisting of individuals who interact with one another.	The capability to leverage resources under the firm's control	Since knowledge underlies capability, advantage always relies somehow on unique knowledge.	Subjectivism

pability refers to "the key role of strategic management in appropriately adapting, integrating and reconfiguring internal and external organizational skills, resources and functional competencies" (Teece et al., 1997, p. 515). Competitive advantage therefore depends on the distinctive processes within the firm (e.g., how it coordinates behaviors), and these, in turn, are governed by the firm's knowledge base and its path-dependent, historical experience (Teece et al., 1997, p. 509).

Thus, as Table 4.3 shows, resource-based theorists put knowledge on a par with other resources. Capability theorists take a more subjectivist approach and argue that resources confer advantage by combining assets with unique, path-dependent skills and knowledge. The latter view synchronizes nicely with a knowledge-based view of competitive advantage and leads to the conclusion that managerial thinking and organizational knowledge should become central constructs in strategic management theory.

Summary

In sum, this chapter was based on the view that strategic renewal involves individual learning, organizational knowledge creation, and knowledge transfer. In the process of our review, we observed at several points that what people know and how they learn are partly a function of the social setting. In the next chapter, we focus more directly on social relationships and the social structures of organizations. The purpose is to better understand how the information exchanged between individuals accumulates as knowledge and leads to the development of organizational capability.

Notes

1. The remaining three properties of sense making are that it is ongoing, that it is focused on and extracted by cues, and that it is driven by plausibility rather than by accuracy.

2. Although they are popular in the management literature, "cause maps" are just one of several different ways to represent managerial cognition. Others include influence diagrams, systems maps, hyper maps, strategic argument mapping and maps of schemas, frames, and linguistic codes. See Huff (1990), pp. 11-49, for a discussion.

3. Recent studies in managerial cognition have broadened their focus to include middle- and operating-level actors (e.g., Balogun & Johnson, 1998; Johnson & Huff, 1998).

4. It is important to note that the supranormal rents generated from employee skills or knowledge must be appropriable by the firm and not the employees themselves. This is more likely when such knowledge is developed within the firm. Consider the difference, for example, between the appropriation of rents generated by Disney's animators (knowledge and skills accumulated within the organization) and by Michael Jordan (innate talent developed mostly independent of the Chicago Bulls).

5 The Social Context
of Strategic Renewal

By virtue of the increased access to information provided in their linking roles, more central midlevel professionals have greater potential to develop a deep sense of the organization's strategic context.

Chapter 3 developed an alternative set of assumptions about the strategy process that redirects researchers attention from a focus on TMT decision making to a focus on the social context within which strategies occur. Rather than being seen as an analytically objective decision process, strategizing is seen as an organizational learning process. From this perspective, new strategies evolve over time, not from discrete decisions but from indeterminate managerial behaviors embedded in a complex social setting. The evolution of future strategy is grounded in existing strategies and competencies that mutate as new information, knowledge, and skills are synthesized and experimented with in organizations.

Understanding strategy from this perspective therefore requires a consideration of the organization's social context. The managerial decisions and actions that guide the evolution of a strategy's development can be seen as rational only within the context in which they are embedded. In this chapter, we review several bodies of theory relevant to social relationships and interaction patterns within organizations. The following section begins with a review of relevant concepts from social network theory. This provides a framework for understanding the *structure* of social relationships. Following this, we introduce notions of trust, politics, and justice to examine the *nature,* or quality, of social relationships.

Social Network Theory

Social network theory, a branch of sociology, has been used to address a variety of issues both within and among organizations. At the interorganizational level, for example, firm environments have been conceived of as "interorganizational fields" composed of transactional relationships among firms that interact (DiMaggio & Powell, 1983). At this level, researchers have used network theory and analysis to explain the strategic conduct of firms, especially their decisions to enter into strategic alliances (Nohria & Eccles, 1992).

At the intraorganizational level, organizations are viewed as "patterns of recurring" relationships among individuals (Lincoln, 1982, p. 26): sets of interdependent roles linked by social networks that transmit information, influence, and affect (Hutt, Reingen, & Ronchetto, 1988). At this level, social network theory holds that individual behaviors occur, and are best understood, within the context of social relationships. The theory is based on the premise that organizations can be usefully conceived of as sets of recurring interaction patterns. Within these patterns, individual actors have regular contact with certain individuals while having little, if any, interaction with others. At the intraorganizational level, network theory has most often been used to explain variations in power and influence among individuals.

Types of Networks

Broadly, network theory is centered around two constructs: nodes (e.g., organizations, individuals) and relationships (e.g., supplier/ buyer, boss/subordinate). Within organizations, the familiar organizational chart depicting the organization's structure provides an illustration of a social network. The chart's boxes, which typically represent functions, positions, or individuals, are the nodes, and the lines between the boxes reflect reporting or communication relationships among the boxes.

Relationships shown on organizational charts represent one dimension of an organization's sociology: formal, or "prescribed," relationships. In addition, organizations include informal, or "emergent" (Ibarra, 1993), relationships that form over time based on friendship, advice, or conversational patterns, often cutting across the organization's formal structure. Organizations, then, are made up of multiple networks (complex combinations of patterned relationships). Researchers studying organizations from this perspective typically have identified and focused on three related types of networks (Tichy, Tushman, & Fombrun, 1979).

Work-Flow Networks

A work-flow network reflects how the organization's overall task is divided. It is created by the exchange of inputs and outputs among organizational members as work flows through the organization and by the resulting interdependencies that develop. Although informal arrangements typically emerge within a work flow, the relationships represented in this type of network are, for the most part, formally prescribed.

Communication Networks

The communication network reflects interdependencies among organizational members created by the exchange of information. Although much of the information transmitted within organizations proceeds through formal channels, much more is transmitted through informal channels, and over time, the efficient operation of most organizations becomes highly dependent on well-established, yet emergent, information conduits.

Friendship Networks

Organizational members are also tied together on the basis of friendship or affect. While clearly not part of the organization's prescribed arrangements, friendship ties may be reflected in the organization's formal design and, importantly, affect emergent communication patterns. Thus, there are significant overlaps among the various types of networks making up an organization.

Research Streams

Within organizations, social network theory has been used to address two related issues: (a) individual differences in organizational power and influence and (b) the influence of social networks on individual attitudes, opinions, and behaviors.

Network Centrality, Power, and Influence

Research on individual influence in organizations has consistently found a relationship between influence and actor centrality in communication (Boje & Whetten, 1981), work-flow (Hinings, Hickson, Pennings, & Schneck, 1974), and friendship networks (Davis, 1969). Theoretically, network centrality increases the potential for influence by creating asymmetrical resource dependencies (Pfeffer & Salancik, 1978). Structural autonomy—the degree to which actors are free to pursue their own goals—is a function of other positions being dependent on a position while that position remains independent of other positions (Burt, 1983). Network centrality increases structural autonomy by providing central actors greater access to information and increased control over information flows. As typically argued, independent access makes central actors less dependent on others, while control creates resource dependencies in others (Brass, 1984).

The fact that network centrality increases actors' access to, and control over, information and resources has clear implications for strategic renewal. By virtue of the increased access to information provided in their linking roles, more central midlevel professionals have greater potential to develop a deep sense of the organization's strategic context. Managers with ties up, down, across, and outside the organization experience the organization from multiple perspectives and, over time, are able to develop an internally consistent understanding of the strategic situation (Floyd & Wooldridge, 1992, 1996). Indeed, while all midlevel personnel do not get access to varied perspectives, a well-positioned midlevel actor may have insights not available to a top manager experiencing the situation from above (Dutton, Ashford, O'Neill, Hayes, & Wierba, 1997; Floyd & Wooldridge, 1996; Walsh, 1995).

In any case, some degree of synthesis is necessary to understand complex strategic realities, and an advantageous network position may therefore be a necessary prerequisite for strategic influence. In addi-

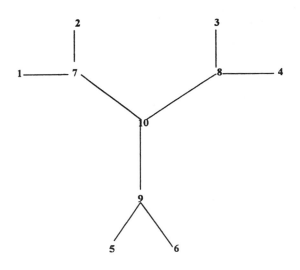

Figure 5.1. Ten-Actor Restricted Access Network

tion, managers who control critical work-flow information or resources may, over time, garner favor with others, gaining their cooperation and support for emergent strategic initiatives (Kanter, 1983). However, while the positive association between actor centrality and power is intuitively logical, empirical research has identified a number of contingencies that potentially influence the strength of this relationship.

Initially, the problem becomes one of determining the appropriate breadth of analysis. "Should centrality within the work group, within the department, or within the entire organization be considered?" (Brass & Burkhardt, 1992, p. 192). Markovsky, Willer, and Patton (1988), for example, found that, within restricted access networks like that shown in Figure 5.1, actors with "local" centrality (e.g., actors 7, 8, and 9) are often more powerful than actors with high "global" centrality (e.g., actor 10). Presumably, this is because, in these networks, locally central actors control needed information and resources through their exclusive ties with peripheral actors (e.g., actors 1, 2, 3, 4, 5, and 6).

Similarly, the centrality-power relationship may be affected by whether the network is "positively" or "negatively" connected (Cook, Emerson, Gillmore, & Yamagishi, 1983). Whereas certain "weak" relationships (Granovetter, 1973) may not have much of an affective component, most recurrent relationships may be characterized as relatively positive or negative. In general, positive relationships have the effect of facilitating information sharing and knowledge transfer across individuals and groups. For example, two positive relations, A-B and B-C, may allow B to obtain information from A that allows B to help C solve a problem. Conversely, negative relations heighten perceptions of intergroup conflict (LaBianca, Brass, & Gray, 1998) and may inhibit or preclude certain other relations. A meeting between A and B, for example, may cause B to cancel a meeting with C.

Using lab experiments, Cook et al. (1983) found that, within "negatively connected" networks, centrality and power are not necessarily associated. In these cases, the relationships of central actors may act as isolating mechanisms, precluding access to information and resources located at the organization's periphery. A special assistant to the CEO, for example, would be considered centrally located. If others perceive the nature of this person's work, or the relationship with the CEO, as threatening, however, the person might become isolated and hold little real influence within the organization. Interestingly, negative connections seem to have a salience that "overwhelms any possible positive effects" (LaBianca et al., 1998, p. 63). Researchers therefore must understand not only the structure of relationships within organizations but also their quality.

A further complication in the centrality-power connection is the multifaceted nature of centrality itself. To be more specific, different actors may exhibit network centrality in different ways. Some, for example, may be central because of their ties with powerful others. Others may be central because they maintain numerous ties throughout the organization. Research investigating the centrality-power thesis therefore must be careful to specify the form of centrality at issue and its theoretical relationship to power. These should be the basis for choosing an appropriate measurement approach.

Freeman (1979) identifies three types of centrality measures: degree, closeness, and betweenness. *Degree* measures of centrality simply count the number of links between an actor and all others and are merely a measure of actor activity within a network. *Closeness* measures indicate how "close" a person is to others in the network and are calculated by summing the lengths of the shortest paths from a given actor to all others in the network. Finally, *betweenness* measures calculate the degree to which actors fall between pairs of actors on the shortest paths connecting them.

Appreciating differences in how alternative centrality measures are related to different forms of influence is important for researchers interested in strategic renewal. Consider, for example, the head of the Radiology Department at a midsize urban hospital who is attempting to get funding for a new piece of capital equipment. From a network perspective, this scenario suggests the importance of centrality in a "closeness" sense. That is, the individual's chances for receiving funding would appear to be increased by having direct links to highly central powerful others in administrative (as opposed to clinical) channels, such as members of the Board of Trustees. Less-direct links involving intermediaries, such as the hospital's chief of staff, may create interdependencies, reduce autonomy, and otherwise place limits on the individual's ability to champion the proposal (Freeman, 1979).

Alternatively, consider the role of facilitating adaptability (Floyd & Wooldridge, 1992). Here, the direction of influence is mostly lateral and downward as an individual encourages others to share information across functional boundaries and experiment with new behaviors. In this case, influence is likely to be enhanced by high "degree" centrality—that is, through numerous direct connections across the organization. These relationships create access to a diverse base of information. Knowing "a little about a lot" is important when the purpose of influence is to broaden the repertoire of organizational responses.

There are, then, distinct theoretical differences in alternative measures of centrality and different types of organizational influence. These contingencies have generated a variety of research findings and raised important issues concerning the centrality-power relationship. At a broader level, however, empirical research continues to support a positive association between an actor's network centrality and his or her power and influence within an organization.

Social Groups and Individual Values, Attitudes, and Opinions

A significant amount of social network research has also focused on the sorting of actors into network subgroups (Mizruchi, 1994). Cohesion or relational approaches group together actors who share strong common relationships to one another. Equivalence or positional models define groups of actors based on common relationships with other actors in the organization. Regardless of the approach, the reasoning for subgrouping is that, theoretically, two individuals with similar social relationships should have similar values, attitudes, and opinions. Both approaches, cohesion and equivalence, have received considerable empirical support in the literature (Mizruchi, 1992, 1993).

Theoretically, then, by identifying and assessing relevant organizational subgroups (social cliques), researchers can predict and explain the attitudes and actions of specific individuals. From a midlevel perspective, for example, such an approach could explain why individuals in one part of the organization, say marketing, support a particular strategy while those in another, such as manufacturing, oppose it. Taken by itself, however, the analysis of social cliques seems limited for understanding how and why a particular manager emerges as a midlevel strategic leader within a group.

Weak Ties and Structural Holes

One approach for addressing the issue of individual influence within a social subgroup stems from Granovetter's (1973) seminal article "The Strength of Weak Ties." As stated by Burt (1992a), the argument is as follows:

> People live in a cluster of others with whom they have strong relations. Information circulates at a high velocity within these clusters. Each person tends to know what the other people know. Therefore, the spread of information on new ideas and opportunities must come through the weak ties that connect people in separate clusters. (p. 72)

The application of this argument to the midlevel perspective appears relatively straightforward. The more weak ties maintained by an individual, the more information he or she has (Galaskiewicz & Wasserman, 1993). Thus, midlevel professionals who maintain diverse inventories of weak ties gain insights into issues and opportunities not apparent to others in similar positions. This asymmetric information creates the opportunity for leadership, allowing certain individuals to shape the awareness of others and influence the direction of adaptive responses.

However, although the weak-tie argument helps explain asymmetric information among middle-level cohorts, weak ties are not an adequate explanation for how middle-level professionals exert strategic influence across cohort groups. Conceptually, the weak-tie construct is meant to represent relationships of relatively weak affect. Weak ties have been measured by (a) the frequency of interactions among individuals, more than once per year but less than twice a week (Granovetter, 1973); (b) the recency of contact (Lin, Dayton, & Greenwald, 1978); and (c) the presence of nonreciprocal nominations (Friedkin, 1980). Regardless of the method, researchers have assumed that weak ties represent relatively shallow relationships in which "liking and trust" have had little opportunity to develop (Krackhardt, 1992). Change, however, is facilitated by strong relationships that include significant "friendship and trust" components (Krackhardt, 1992). Krackhardt and Stern (1988), for example, demonstrated the pattern of friendship ties across departmental boundaries to be associated with the organization's ability to adapt to environmental change and uncertainty.

Thus, it appears that weak ties provide certain middle-level professionals with information not commonly shared by others in their cohort group. This information provides these individuals with insights, allowing them to exert influence within their group. Weak ties alone, however, do not explain how certain middle-level professionals emerge as leaders influencing strategic change across social cliques. For this level of influence, theory and research suggest that the importance of affect-based relationships centered around friendship and trust.

Recognizing that the weak-tie construct directs attention to the strength of the relationship rather than its location, Burt (1992b) develops the alternative construct of structural holes. In essence, a structural hole reflects the lack of a relationship or tie between individual actors in different social cliques or between entire social cliques. A relationship that "bridges" these holes generates information benefits regardless of whether the tie is strong or weak. Thus, the construct more directly captures the causal agent of information asymmetry (Burt, 1992b). Importantly, however, as Burt (1992a) notes, "weak-tie bridges are more likely than strong-tie bridges" (p. 74). Granovetter (1973), in fact, argues that strong-tie bridges are so unlikely that they are virtually nonexistent: "[T]hough they [weak ties] are not automatically bridges.

Table 5.1   Relevant Constructs From Social Network Theory

Construct	Definition	Significance to Midlevel Theory
Actor centrality	Degree to which various communications flow to and from an individual actor	Increases an actor's potential for influence within the organization
Social cliques	Degree to which individuals share similar social relationships	Isolates the location of knowledge and information within the organization
Bridging relationships	Idiosyncratic relationships that link otherwise unconnected groups or individuals	Explains individual knowledge differences among structurally equivalent actors; promotes the migration of knowledge across organizational units

What is important is that all bridges are weak ties" (p. 1064). Burt (1992a) counters, however, arguing that the "strategic player" focusing on the maintenance of bridge ties can keep bridges from falling "into their natural state of being weak ties" (p. 75). The extant literature, then, recognizes the possibility of strong, affect-based, bridging relationships. It is these relationships that would seem to provide an individual with the opportunity to facilitate strategic change.

In sum, as shown in Table 5.1, the notions of actor centrality, social cliques, and bridging relationships hold important implications for a middle-level perspective of strategy making. Various forms of network centrality increase actors' potential for alternative types of influence within the organization. Social cliques, whether equivalence- or cohesion-based, suggest that strategic information is housed within specific locations within an organization. Viewing strategy as a puzzle, the implication is that pieces of the puzzle (bits of strategic information) are "locked" inside separate locations. Bridging relationships that span social cliques provide the key to uniting these disparate pieces of information. Weak bridging relationships, however, only provide for a sharing of information and may not facilitate strategic change across groups. In most cases, then, the influence of midlevel professionals will be bounded within social cliques. Influence across cliques will be relatively rare, and garnering such influence will likely require the pro-active management and nurturing of bridging relationships.

Trust: The Foundation of Cooperation

Although social network analysis helps describe the structure of social relationships in organizations, the approach is relatively silent, both conceptually and as a method, in helping one understand the content or nature of key relationships. This limitation is recognized in Krackhardt's (1992) observations on the importance of *philos* in bridging relationships. *Philos,* roughly translated from Greek as friendship, is important in facilitating organizational change, Krackhardt maintains. Weak ties (Granovetter, 1974) may be important as novel information sources, but *philos,* or strong affect-based relationships, is critical in motivating actors to take risks.

Krackhardt's (1992) arguments are supported and reflected in current discussions of trust within the organizational sciences (Rousseau, Sitkin, Burt, & Camerer, 1998). Mutual trust is a predominant quality underlying *philos*-based relationships (Krackhardt, 1992). More fundamentally, trust is the key element that allows societies and organizations to function (Barnard, 1938; Tyler & Kramer, 1996). Without some level of trust, even the most limited form of cooperation is difficult to explain (Deutsch, 1958). Therefore, trust is central in ongoing social relationships, and the notion of trust is clearly relevant to a socially based theory of strategizing. In the following section, we present a basic definition of *trust* and describe its centrality to strategizing.

The Centrality of Trust

Trust has long been recognized as a fundamental feature of interpersonal and collective behavior, and numerous definitions of *trust* have appeared in the literature (Hosmer, 1995; Tyler & Kramer, 1996). Common among most definitions is the notion that trust is the expectation or confidence that one party holds about the intentions or likely actions of another. Succinctly, when we trust someone, we believe that he or she will not unfairly exploit our vulnerabilities. We may then choose to interact or cooperate with this individual in a manner that opens us up to possible exploitation.

Within the organizational sciences, scholars, for the most part, have viewed trust as an alternative control or governance mechanism (Bromiley & Cummings, 1992; Lorenz, 1988). From this perspective, the costs of formal planning, monitoring, and control systems are viewed as transactions costs associated with the organization's employment of personnel. Higher levels of trust are seen as lowering these transactions costs, because presumably the cost of monitoring a trustworthy individual is less than that of monitoring a nontrustworthy one.

The Multidimensionality of the Trust Concept

Because it is a familiar concept, it is easy to take the definition of *trust* for granted. It is not surprising, therefore, that early treatments of trust in the organizational literature left the term's meaning somewhat ambiguous (Barber, 1983; Luhmann, 1988). More recently, scholars have distinguished trust from its behavioral results (e.g., cooperation or delegation; Mishra, 1996) and have identified the essential conditions underlying its occurrence (Butler & Cantrell, 1984; Hosmer, 1995).

Using a review of the trust literature and interviews with practicing managers, Mishra (1996) arrives at the following definition: *"Trust is one party's willingness to be vulnerable to another party based on the belief that the latter party is (a) competent, (b) open, (c) concerned, and (d) reliable"* (p. 262).

Mishra's dimensions (competence, openness, concern, and reliability) parallel elements identified by others (Butler & Cantrell, 1984; Gabarro, 1978) and represent a parsimonious framework explicating the trust construct. Table 5.2 summarizes these dimensions and possible implications for strategic renewal.

Each dimension—competence, openness, concern, and reliability—has its own effect on the level of trust that develops between two individuals, within a work group, or in an organization. For the most part, each is necessary but insufficient to achieving high levels of trust. We may have a high degree of confidence in a leader's ability (competence), for example, but if we do not believe she is concerned for our interest, we will not trust her. Thus, the dimensions are not compensatory with one another; that is, a high level of one does not make up for a low level

Table 5.2   The Dimensions of Trust

Mishra's (1996) Dimensions of Trust	Definition	Significance to Midlevel Theory
Competence	One can have confidence in both the behavior of another and any resulting shared outcomes because the individual is viewed as qualified or proficient.	Potential participants in a midlevel initiative base decisions to participate at least partially on their perceptions of the competence of the central actor and other participants.
Openness	One can be trusted because he or she is mentally accessible (i.e., willing to share ideas and information freely and honestly with others).	Midlevel actors are more likely to cooperate with an emerging initiative when they feel that information is being fully shared and disclosed.
Concern/Integrity/ Loyalty	Belief that one will not be taken advantage of by another because the other is genuinely concerned, loyal, and/or a person of integrity or principle.	Midlevel actors will be more likely to cooperate with an emerging initiative when they feel that they share a common interest with other participants.
Reliability/ Consistency	One can be trusted because of the consistency observed between his or her words and past behaviors.	Trust builds over time as the result of interactions and key events.

of another. Methodologically, this suggests that the dimensions combine multiplicatively (Mishra, 1996). That is, if one were to measure trust by assessing perceived levels of each of the four dimensions, the overall level of trust would be best represented by the *product,* not the sum, of the dimensions' individual scores. In this way, a low level in one area would translate into an overall low level of trust.

Levels of Trust

In addition to various dimensions of trust, researchers have developed various classification schemes to identify different levels of trust. Barney and Hansen (1994), for example, in their discussion of trustworthiness, describe weak, semistrong, and strong forms of trust. Here,

Table 5.3   Lewicki and Bunker's Stagewise Evolution of Trust

Trust Level	Definition	Significance to Midlevel Theory
Calculus-based	Deterrence-based trust: Individuals will do what they say because they fear the consequences of not doing so.	It is unlikely that midlevel actors will cooperate on risky projects that have no official sanction.
Knowledge-based	Predictability-based trust: The behavior of individuals is anticipatable from what is known about their past behavior.	Voluntary cooperation among midlevel actors will be governed by perceptions of other actors' motivations and likely behaviors.
Identification-based	Sharing-based trust: Behavior can be anticipated as the individuals share the same needs, choices, and preferences.	Autonomous midlevel activity is facilitated by a sharing of common values and motivations.

each form is based on a different rationale, or reason to trust. Weak-form trust, for instance, is based on a condition of limited vulnerability. That is, parties trust one another because the relationship opens them up to few, if any, potentially negative consequences. Semistrong trust, on the other hand, is based on a governance structure that imposes various kinds of costs on individuals or groups who behave opportunistically. Trust in one's suppliers, for example, may be based on conditions and recourses specified in a contract. Within organizations, semistrong trust is akin to the type of "trust" that managers hold for employees who are controlled through formal systems. Finally, Barney and Hansen's strong-form trust is based on "values, principles, and standards of behavior that have been internalized by the parties" (p. 179). Here, parties trust one another based on the history of their past interactions and on assumptions they hold concerning the values and standards of the other.

Barney and Hansen's model suggests that only under conditions of strong-form trust will the kinds of autonomous strategic behaviors necessary for renewal occur. By definition, induced behaviors are prescribed by the organization's planning and control systems. In contrast, autonomous midlevel behaviors require individuals to act voluntarily, to exert effort, and to assume risks in a project with ambiguous outcomes. Only under conditions in which individuals both trust others and feel trusted, absent formal governance, are these behaviors likely to occur.

That midlevel strategic initiative requires strong-form trust returns us to questions of how it occurs within organizations. Addressing this question, Lewicki and Bunker (1996) develop a hierarchy of trust and assert that, under normal conditions, trust develops over time proceeding from weaker to stronger forms. Table 5.3 summarizes Lewicki and Bunker's stagewise evolution of trust.

Calculus-Based Trust

Shapiro, Sheppard, and Cheraskin (1992) identified deterrence-based trust as a consistency of behavior that is assured through the fear of sanctions or consequences. Lewicki and Bunker (1996) expand this definition to include rewards associated with trustworthy behavior. That is, in this form of trust, actors "calculate" the rewards and punishments associated with both trustworthy and opportunistic behavior. They act in a trustworthy manner when they believe that doing so serves their self-interest, through either the receipt of rewards or the avoidance of punishments. Calculus-based trust, then, is akin to Barney and Hansen's semistrong form of trust, and it relies on exogenous factors such as governance mechanisms to ensure trustworthy behavior.

Knowledge-Based Trust

The next higher form of trust, knowledge-based trust, is rooted in the parties' knowing each other sufficiently well so that behaviors can be reliably anticipated and predicted. At this level, trust is endogenous, embedded in a social history of regular interactions and communications. Somewhat paradoxically, trust at this level may be enhanced when others' behaviors are predictably untrustworthy. For example, a person who is predictably late does not violate others' trust when he or she comes to a meeting 15 minutes after its scheduled start (Lewicki &

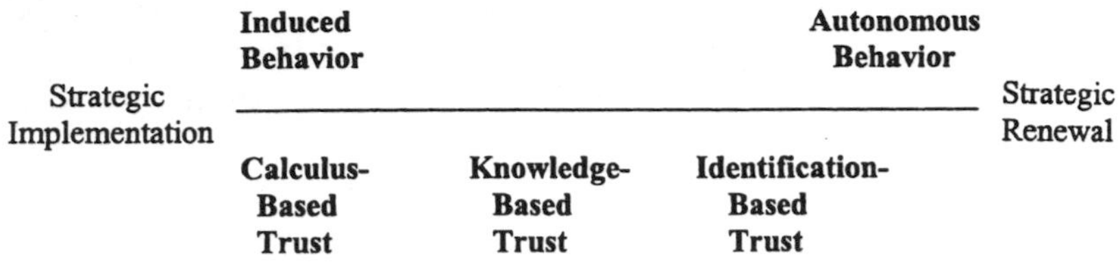

	Induced Behavior		Autonomous Behavior	
Strategic Implementation	_____			Strategic Renewal
	Calculus-Based Trust	Knowledge-Based Trust	Identification-Based Trust	

Figure 5.2. The Relationship Between Midlevel Behavior and Levels of Organizational Trust

Bunker, 1996). In this case, knowledge of the person's regular behavior, inconsiderate as it may be, allows others to trust the situation, knowing that the person will eventually get to the meeting.

Identification-Based Trust

Lewicki and Bunker's strongest form, identification-based trust, occurs as individuals begin to share common desires and motivations. Kramer (1993), for example, describes how cooperation is advanced in organizations when members come to identify with, and ascribe similar importance to, the organization's goals. In these cases, trusting parties not only possess a knowledge of one another but share common priorities and objectives as well. "Identification-based trust thus permits a party to serve as the other's agent and substitute for the other in interpersonal transactions" (Lewicki & Bunker, 1996, p. 122).

Stronger forms of trust are embedded in a history of ongoing social relationships, and the development of trust proceeds from weaker to stronger forms over time. Trust between two interacting parties, for example, may become knowledge-based after a period of time when there are few, if any, calculus-based infringements. Similarly, knowledge-based trust may evolve into identification-based trust as parties learn more about one another and come to see others' priorities, needs, and goals as their own.

It is not surprising that interest in trust as an organizational attribute has risen as increased numbers of firms have adopted more process-based arrangements (Creed & Miles, 1996). The notion of trust as a necessary condition underlying self-organizing coordination points to the centrality of trust in strategic renewal. The emergence of divergent strategic initiatives from within an organization depends on actors in the organization cooperating in ways that are not officially sanctioned, or mandated by formal arrangements. Initiatives develop when peers from around the organization volunteer various resources and skills to an unproven, unofficial endeavor. As shown in Figure 5.2, therefore, low levels of trust are likely to limit an organization's ability to realize strategic renewal.

Trust and the Political Nature of the Strategy Process

Building on the work of others (MacMillan, 1978; Pettigrew, 1973; Quinn, 1978), Narayanan and Fahey (1982) describe strategy formation as a political process that resolves inherent conflict arising from multiple competing interests through bargaining and negotiation. They argue that strategies result from the interplay among temporary coalitions that form in support of or in opposition to specific issues and initiatives. More specifically, they describe a five-stage model consisting of activation, mobilization, coalescence, encounter, and decision. The first stage, activation, is triggered as individuals begin to recognize important issues or concerns[1] and is completed when "individuals have developed a sufficient level of clarity and a 'language' about their concerns to be able to articulate the issues . . . to other organizational members" (Narayanan & Fahey, 1982, p. 28). In the second stage, mobilization, a shared awareness of the issue(s) begins to develop among various organizational members. As awareness builds, individuals begin to mobilize and develop alliances with others who share similar concerns and interests. By the third stage, coalescence, the need for action to resolve the issue has become increasingly apparent; in response, a coalition emerges that is committed to resolving the issue in a specific way.

During the first three stages, then, which Narayanan and Fahey (1982) collectively label the gestation period, a coalition emerges in support of a specific strategic initiative. In the fourth stage, encounter, the coalition begins to champion its initiative, attempting to "sell it" to other individuals, coalitions, and subunits within the organization. This stage is marked by "bilateral negotiations" across groups and is often characterized by conflict that emerges as the positions of various groups and individuals become increasingly clear and solidified. Finally, in the last stage, the issue is resolved through a "strategic decision."

The characterization of strategy formation as a political process is consistent with a middle-level perspective and further highlights the centrality of trust in the process. The formation of coalitions in support of specific initiatives requires individuals to accept heightened degrees of vulnerability. Coalition members often pool resources and allow other members of the coalition to represent their positions. Membership within coalitions is based on "an awareness of *likeness* on the part of members and an awareness of *differences* or estrangement from others" (Narayanan & Fahey, 1982, p. 30). Still, members of coalitions have important differences (Cyert & March, 1963) that to some degree can be resolved through intracoalition bargaining but that ultimately must be reconciled through the emergence of mutual trust. Similarly, although many differences across coalitions can be resolved through compromise, "side payments," and so on, in the end, a general lack of trust will inhibit the process. Indeed, individuals are unlikely to attend to issues and begin the process at all when they believe that doing so will evoke retaliation by others (Narayanan & Fahey, 1982).

Trust as a Contextual Variable

Until this point, trust has been discussed as a quality describing the nature of a relationship between two or more parties. In this sense, each dyad or line connecting individual nodes in a social network can be described in terms of its level of trust. Social interactions occur within a broader context, however, and notions of trust also describe qualities underlying work-group and organizational environments. At this level, notions of justice, or perceived fairness, have become prominent in the literature. Broadly, theories of justice make predictions about how people will react to various outcomes and processes within organizations based on the degree to which they are perceived to be just or fair. Equity theory, for example, holds that people judge the fairness of the rewards they receive by comparing them with the rewards that others receive.

Theories of justice fall into two general categories. Notions of distributive justice hold that workers' attitudes are shaped by the degree to which they believe that rewards are fairly and equitably distributed within organizations. Alternatively, procedural justice focuses on the degree to which parties believe in the integrity and fairness of the processes used to allocate rewards. Past research (Folger & Konovsky, 1989; Greenberg, 1986) has shown these forms of justice to be correlated with one another and to be important in shaping employees' attitudes and behaviors.

More recently, research (Sweeney & McFarlin, 1993) has shown perceptions of procedural fairness to be more closely associated with global evaluations of organizations (e.g., organizational commitment) and perceptions of distributive fairness to be more closely related to personal-level evaluations (e.g., pay satisfaction). Intuitively, both forms of justice seem related to how willing an individual might be to exert extra (voluntary) effort in support of a midlevel initiative. At the personal level, when actors are dissatisfied with their standing in the organization, they may be less focused on strategic issues. In these cases, a focus on self-interest may become acute. Alternatively, issues of procedural justice are likely to affect actors' perceptions of the likelihood of the long-term accomplishment of fair outcomes (Lind & Tyler, 1988), and this may affect their willingness to attend to strategic issues, initiate proposals, join coalitions, or otherwise engage in voluntary strategy-enhancing behavior.

Summary

Social network theory provides a technology and set of constructs that allow researchers to understand and assess the *structure* of social relationships. Complementing this, the literatures on trust within organizations, the political nature of strategic decision making, and issues of perceived fairness or justices within organizations provide the background for assessing relationship *quality*.

Chapters 4 and 5 have reviewed theory and research relevant to a conceptualization of strategy formation as a social learning process. In a broad sense, we believe that the constructs and theory underlying these bodies of literature are applicable to strategy process research whether or not one takes a middle-level perspective. In Part 3, we draw on these bodies of literature to develop our ideas about middle-level strategy process research. Chapter 6 presents a middle-level model of strategic renewal. Chapter 7 identifies high-priority issues and discusses appropriate research approaches. Readers will note that, in taking a middle-level perspective, we do not focus on middle-level managers to the exclusion of others. Indeed, some of our propositions are about top managers. More to the point, our perspective is that, because the information flows and interactions necessary for social learning occur at the organization's middle, theory and research should focus there. Stated differently, the middle is where actors from throughout the organization come together to create strategy.

Note

1. The authors note that the extent to which individuals focus on specific issues "is a function of: (1) perceived salience of issues; (2) extent of competing claims on the individual's time and resources; (3) political factors such as anticipated retaliatory actions by others; and (4) perceived ability to initiate actions, fear of failure and consequent loss of credibility" (Narayanan & Fahey, 1982, p. 28).

III

A Middle-Level Perspective

6 A Middle-Level Model of
Strategic Renewal

Managers in the middle are the "clutch" of strategic renewal.

Taken together, what implications do the theories and constructs reviewed in previous chapters hold for a middle-level view of strategic renewal? How does a middle-level perspective fit into the overall domain of strategy research? In this chapter, we use the ideas in the previous two chapters (on organizational knowledge, social networks, and trust) to describe the renewal process from a middle-level perspective. As we begin, however, it is important to recognize explicitly the complex nature of the processes we are attempting to depict.

In Chapter 3, we developed an alternative set of assumptions to guide strategy process research. In particular, we argued that *"New capabilities emerge from socially complex processes that are embedded in existing knowledge and social relationships."* This is a key assumption. It is the complexity of the capability-building process that makes it difficult for others to imitate organizational capabilities and erode competitive advantages.

Building on this assumption and the framework presented in the introduction, this chapter describes three *process* capabilities that underlie strategic renewal. We discuss how these are interconnected in a complex system. Then, in the heart of the chapter, we present our model of strategic renewal. By linking capability development back to the litera-

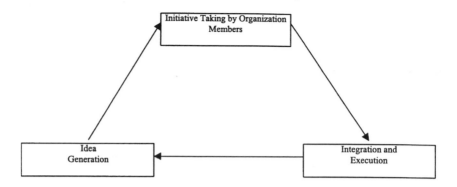

Figure 6.1. Elements of Strategic Renewal

ture in previous chapters, we describe strategic renewal in a way that suggests practical avenues for empirical research. This sets the stage for the discussion of high-priority research issues in Chapter 7.

Strategic Renewal
as a Complex System

As shown in Figure 6.1, our conceptualization of strategic renewal includes three interrelated processes: idea generation, initiative development, and strategic reintegration. Our assumption is that some degree of capability in all three of these domains is a prerequisite to strategic renewal. Each element represents an identifiable phase of the evolutionary process (variation, selection, and retention). From a middle-level perspective, each also brackets a long succession of social interactions among many individuals within and outside the organization.

Figure 6.1 shows the three components of strategic renewal as interrelated sequential subprocesses. In reality, however, the relationships among these elements are more complex. At any point in time, all three may be occurring simultaneously. Furthermore, as we shall see, each subprocess is itself a complex combination of interactions. Still, their dependence on one another is important because each one appears to be associated with a different set of norms, values, and organizational arrangements. Thus, strategic renewal requires organizations to create and manage highly differentiated tasks with potentially conflicting priorities.

The sequence in the figure also shows that renewal is evolutionary, and the three subprocesses mirror the variation, selection, and retention stages of the evolutionary cycle (Burgelman, 1983b, 1983c, 1991). Adaptive renewal requires the generation of divergent ideas in sufficient number and quality, the selection of some of these over others based on their fit with the strategic context, and the retention of adaptive initiatives in the form of formal structures and organizational routines. Characterizing renewal in this way does not rule out deliberate efforts on the part of management to facilitate organizational learning (Hamel & Prahalad, 1989). It does, however, point to the importance of adaptive search (Levinthal & March, 1993), emergent adaptation (Mintzberg, 1978), and other unintentional kinds of learning.

In addition, the interdependence of the subprocesses has implications for the organization's ongoing capability development process. In particular, by arguing that integration and execution are precursors to the idea-generation process, we are recognizing that the emergence of divergent ideas within the organization cannot be separated from prior experience and organizational memory (Huber, 1991; Teece, Pisano, & Shuen, 1997; Weick, 1995). Structural holes and weak social ties may penetrate the organization's boundaries, but, once absorbed, new information becomes intertwined with existing knowledge. It gets framed and interpreted in light of what people already know (Dearborn & Simon, 1958; Dutton, Fahey, & Narayanan, 1983; Dutton & Jackson, 1987). This increases the possibility that discrepant ideas will be discounted and that what is learned will be seen to reinforce what is already known (Levinthal & March, 1993). Yet without a base of domain-specific knowledge, it is difficult to absorb new ideas in a given arena (Cohen & Levinthal, 1990). Thus, the relationship between new ideas and existing knowledge appears to create a paradox. In order to learn, organizations must already know something about a given subject, but the existence of such knowledge can impede the organization's ability to learn from new ideas (Huff, Huff, & Thomas, 1992; Leonard-Barton, 1992). In the next section, we suggest a way out of this paradox by examining each subprocess in detail, drawing specific connections with the theory described in Chapters 4 and 5.

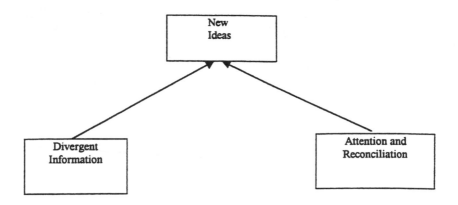

Figure 6.2. The Emergence of Strategically Divergent Ideas

The Generation
of New Ideas

Figure 6.2 presents a framework for understanding the emergence of strategically divergent ideas within organizations. In brief, the figure is meant to show that new ideas are generated by individuals who (a) have access to strategically relevant divergent information and (b) are motivated to attend to and reconcile divergent information with existing knowledge.

Theory and research suggest that new ideas emanate from one or two individuals (Floyd & Wooldridge, 1999; Narayanan & Fahey, 1982; Nonaka, 1994). While obvious, this starting point is important because it provides the beginning of an explanation for how organizations learn to extend their knowledge in ways that diverge from the dominant belief system.

Each individual carries around within his or her head a subjectively valid set of beliefs. The potential for individual subjectivity within organizations, therefore, means that acceptance of an idea is contingent on the idea's consistency with an *individual's* belief system—not the ideology of the organization as a whole. Compared with empirical or pragmatic criteria, which may apply on other occasions, subjective criteria require only that one person believe in an idea. Subjectivity therefore opens up the organization to influence from individual "gut feel."

A subjective idea need not be well formulated or articulated to be accepted, and as a result, tacit or implicit knowledge may leak into the organization through the intuitions of individual members.

    P1:   *Divergent ideas and implicit knowledge are accepted into the*
            organization through the subjective belief systems of individuals.

Because such insights are unfettered by externally imposed empirical or pragmatic criteria, it is more likely that organization members will come to believe in ideas that diverge from the organizational ideology. Despite this potential, however, truly divergent ideas are often difficult to cultivate. Indeed, it has long been known that new beliefs are tied to past beliefs. Over time, we learn "what works" and develop routines reflecting this. With the passage of time, individuals and organizations tend to get better and better doing fewer and fewer things (Nelson, 1991). Learning becomes highly focused on incremental improvements in existing routines (Levinthal & March, 1993). Organizational experiences, including tenure in a functional unit, promote narrow belief systems whose concerns are limited to current goals and activities (Cyert & March, 1963; Dearborn & Simon, 1958; Stagner, 1969; Weick, 1979). More generally, cognitive psychologists have found that established mental maps become mental "traps," preventing us from perceiving the novelty in a given situation (Huff, 1990). In other words, what has been learned so far, our existing knowledge, prevents us from learning or even recognizing alternative logics.

Thus, the generation of ideas that have potential to initiate truly new directions is highly problematic. Tempered somewhat by the degree of organizational slack (Bourgeois & Singh, 1983), the thoughts of most organizational members are focused around ongoing routines. Divergent ideas, to the extent that they exist at all, start as the subjective, even iconoclastic, perspectives of one or a very few individuals. How, then, do certain individuals begin to think beyond the current strategy?

Accessing Strategic Information

There are many theories to explain individual creativity. In researching the entrepreneurial success of European minorities, Glade (1967) offers an intriguing sociological explanation that can be linked to the

social psychological processes involved in strategic renewal. Specifically, Glade's research shows that the beliefs and perceptions of socially deviant groups are markedly different from those of the majority
population. These differences evolve to a greater or lesser degree depending on the extent of isolation from mainstream society. It is important to note that, for our purposes, the differences in beliefs identified by Glade include differences in perceived entrepreneurial
opportunities. In other words, divergent entrepreneurial ideas emanate from "deviant" perspectives, belief systems that differ significantly
from the dominant ideology.

A similar phenomenon may exist in organizational settings. Like mi-
nority populations, certain individuals in organizations appear to believe in opportunities that are unknown or unacceptable to others. The
difference, however, is that these divergent ideas—if they are to be at all
useful to the organization—must ultimately gain broader acceptance.
Therefore, the emergence of divergent ideas that can be eventually integrated back into the broader purpose appears to depend on the existence of individuals whose social position is somehow isolated yet also
connected to the organization. This is where social network theory can
be applied to make Glade's deviance theory of entrepreneurship fit the
organizational context.

We have already seen how the existence of weak ties provides individuals with exposure to divergent information (Burt, 1992a; Granovetter,
1973). Weak ties channel information from social relationships that
are outside the bonds of friendship and trust in the formal organization. However, the information asymmetries created by weak ties isolate certain individuals and differentiate their knowledge from others
within the group. As discussed here, knowledge is accepted true belief
(i.e., something considered to be true). Differences in information create the "deviance effect" by altering people's perceptions and beliefs. In
short, individuals who establish and maintain bridging relationships
are likely to have somewhat deviant mind-sets. But, unlike ethnic minorities who often remain isolated, in an organizational setting, devi-
ants may also enjoy relationships that connect them to the dominant
group. As Stacey (1995) argues, "Weak ties . . . provide 'bridges' to other
parts of a social system through which variety may be imported into a
cluster of people held together by strong ties"[1] (p. 489).

> P2:   *Weak ties are a primary source of divergent information that creates*
>   *information asymmetries between organization members.*

> P3:   Information asymmetries differentiate the knowledge of individuals
>   from that of other organization members.

Reconciling Divergent and Existing Information

Even though weak ties provide individuals with unique knowledge, the arguments till this point do not address what causes individuals to pay attention to strategic issues in the first place. That is, why do individuals attach strategic meaning to information provided by weak ties? Thinking about the implications of new information requires cognitive effort, and individuals are unlikely to expend this effort unless there is a sufficient motivation to do so.

In this regard, a minimum requirement would seem to be the individual's concern over some aspect of current strategy. In other words, the individual would need to be knowledgeable enough about the firm's established strategy (and emergent events) to form a critical evaluation. Only a knowledgeable individual, one capable of thinking critically about the logic underlying strategy, would recognize the strategic salience of new information and, hence, expend the effort necessary to reconcile the new information with existing logic. Thus, new ideas are likely to emanate from individuals who are both separated from and connected to the dominant mind-set.

> P4:   Individuals who are knowledgeable about the existing strategy are
>   more likely to attend to the organizational implications of new
>   information provided through weak ties.

In addition to knowledge about existing strategy, individuals are not likely to consider an idea relevant to their role in the organization unless they believe they have the potential to influence the organization with their ideas (Lyles & Mitroff, 1980). This sense of personal power develops when people experience a sense of control over their behavior. Thus, Nonaka (1994) argues that autonomy "widens the possibility that individuals will motivate themselves to form new [organizational] knowledge" (p. 18).

> P5:   Individuals who have sufficient autonomy to influence the
>   organization are more likely to be motivated to think about the
>   organizational implications of an idea.

Finally, political considerations may influence an individual's motivation to develop new ideas (Narayanan & Fahey, 1982). An individual whose attention is dominated by an awareness of various self-interests within the organization is less likely to attend to strategic concerns. New ideas bring change and inevitably alter organizational arrangements. Thus, individuals who are acutely sensitive to the established self-interests of others—or worse, who fear retaliation by others—are unlikely to consider divergent ideas as either legitimate or desirable options.

> P6:   Individuals with an acute awareness of political concerns within the organization are unlikely to be the source of new, divergent ideas.

In sum, the subjective divergent ideas of individuals represent sources of new and often implicit organizational knowledge. Such knowledge is created when (a) individuals accept beliefs on the basis of intuition or other subjective criteria unconnected to the organizational ideology and (b) they are connected by bridging relationships to deviant sources of information. Subjectivity and weak social ties thus skirt the tendency of organizations to learn more and more about existing routines and ignore divergent ideas. Finally, it is the individuals' motivation to believe in new ideas that begins the process of strategic renewal.

From Ideas to Initiatives

The second subprocess of strategic renewal moves from concept to initiative. Emergent strategic initiatives may be defined as autonomous efforts within a group to affect significant change in organizational capability (Burgelman, 1983b). As noted above, such initiatives have been identified as the building blocks of strategic renewal, and the concept has been featured prominently in evolutionary models of strategic change (Burgelman, 1983b, 1991; Hart, 1992; Huff et al., 1992). Initiatives that originate at middle or operating levels of the hierarchy have also been identified as a unit of analysis in research on innovation (Kanter, 1982), new product development (Leonard-Barton, 1992), and new venture development (Burgelman, 1983c). In the broadest sense, these initiatives can be understood as a source of emergent strategy (Mintzberg, 1978).

The activities comprising emergent strategic initiatives are familiar. They generally begin with an individual who is motivated to "sell" his or her idea to another organization member (Dutton & Ashford, 1993; Kanter, 1983). This often leads to the collection and analysis of additional information relevant to key issues and concerns. Other specific activities in later stages of an initiative include pilot projects, trial runs, prototypes, and other forms of experimentation. In most instances, inputs from a variety of organizational functions (e.g., engineering drawings, process studies, costing, market research, etc.) are incorporated in the process of developing an initiative.

Before describing the initiative development process in more detail, it is important to differentiate between emergent strategic initiatives and other kinds of initiatives. First, not all emergent initiatives are *strategic* initiatives. Many represent incremental improvements to products, processes, or services. Strategic initiatives, however, have the potential to change core organizational capabilities and thereby shift the basis of competitive advantage. These initiatives imply significant change in the organization's knowledge and skill base, its technical and administrative systems, its norms and values, or all three at once (Leonard-Barton, 1992). Such initiatives are divergent because they imply significant change in how the organization competes.

Second, some initiatives start with approval or encouragement from top management (Quinn, 1980). Many of these initiatives are not emergent, however, in the sense that they do not depart from top management intent (Mintzberg & Waters, 1985) and are unlikely to diverge from official strategy (Burgelman, 1994). Thus, although they may be considered part of incremental strategy formulation (Quinn, 1980), induced strategic initiatives are outside the scope of the present theory.

The Development of Emergent Strategic Initiatives

Figure 6.3 identifies four developmental processes associated with emergent strategic initiatives: interpretation, articulation, elaboration, and ratification. Each of these plays a role in explaining how ideas are transformed into organizational capability. The figure also depicts the key factors associated with the developmental processes and the corresponding propositions in the model.

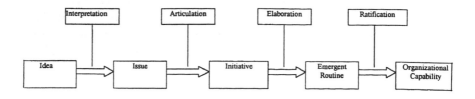

Figure 6.3. The Development of Emergent Strategic Initiatives

As the figure shows, emergent strategic initiatives are born when a middle manager's interpretation of an idea links it to a strategic issue facing the organization. Issues, in turn, become initiatives when an informal social network forms around a central actor, who is also frequently a middle manager. As the middle manager articulates the idea in interactions with others, the tacit or subjective knowledge associated with the original idea becomes more explicit. This reduces the initiative's reliance on a single actor and facilitates the elaboration of the emergent social network across various functions and hierarchical levels within the organization. Cooperation among subunits in the performance of trial runs, pilot projects, and the like triggers a reconsideration of existing functional-level knowledge and a reconfiguration of patterns of coordination between subunits. This leads to the development of new procedural knowledge in the form of emergent organization routines. Before these routines may become part of the organization's operating capabilities, the initiative must be ratified by top management. Ratification involves both substantive links to official strategy and process links to political dynamics within top management.

Interpretation: The Genesis of Emergent Strategic Initiatives

Early on, divergent ideas with the potential to become emergent strategic initiatives are merely tentative beliefs held by one or two people. The underlying facts and core logic therefore remain subjective. Accepted on the basis of simple consistency with the beliefs of one or two people, both the social and substantive scope of the idea are quite narrow. The belief is untested by dialogue and unchallenged by debate, and awareness of the idea in the organization is virtually nil. No one in the organization—probably including the idea generator—sees the idea as relevant to strategy. Thus, from an organizational point of view, the knowledge associated with the idea is subjective, tacit, and incomplete.

To get beyond this point, for an idea to develop into a strategic initiative, someone must be willing to associate it with a significant strategic issue and/or promote it as a solution to an important problem facing the organization (Kanter, 1982). In the process, the idea-become-issue is redefined by incorporating new perspectives and interests (Dutton & Jackson, 1987; Narayanan & Fahey, 1982). Research suggests that the individual who first has the idea is not likely to be the one to recognize it as a strategic issue or to champion it within the corporation (Venkataraman, MacMillan, & McGrath, 1992). This shift in actors from idea generator to issue seller may be because of a lack of communication skills. Equally as likely, it results from the isolation created by the idea generator's "deviant" mind-set and unique set of social relationships (Granovetter, 1973; Stacey, 1995).

Often, it is middle managers who play the "pivotal role in detecting new ideas and in mobilizing resources around these new ideas" (Dutton, Ashford, O'Neill, Hayes, & Wierba, 1997, p. 407). Those in the middle are in a unique position to link divergent ideas to strategic issues—having access both to operating-level information about customers, technologies, and so forth and to top management's strategic priorities (Floyd & Wooldridge, 1992, 1997). This unique "linking pin" pattern of relationships makes top management dependent on middle managers for critical information about strategic alternatives and the effectiveness of particular strategies. Middle managers use upward influence to present their interpretation of strategic issues to top management (Floyd & Wooldridge, 1992). The effect is to give middle managers a significant role in determining what top managers pay attention to and thereby in shaping the organization's strategic agenda (Dutton & Ashford, 1993).

Thus, being immersed in the world of strategy and operations, middle managers are likely to recognize the strategic potential of an idea. From a purely cognitive perspective, their personal belief system is more likely than others to integrate higher-order concepts (e.g., competitive strategy) with lower-order concepts (e.g., an idea for a new technology). In this way, middle managers' perspective can be seen to mediate between the conceptual knowledge of strategy and the concrete operating knowledge contained in a particular idea (Senge, 1996). Middle management's interpretations thus serve as both filter (screening out) and funnel (drawing in) for the process of transforming divergent ideas into strategic issues.

> P7:   *Middle managers' cognitive perspective makes it likely that they will associate divergent ideas with strategic issues and that their interpretation will provide the impetus for emergent strategic initiatives.*

Issue Articulation and Emergent Social Networks

So far, we have argued that middle managers' cognitive framework makes them crucial in bringing attention to divergent ideas as strategic issues. Picking up divergent ideas from subordinates, peers, or superiors and championing them in a strategic context is a natural part of middle managers' role as synthesizers and issue sellers. Although these autonomous strategic processes have been identified in prior work (e.g., Bower, 1970; Burgelman, 1983b; Dutton et al., 1997; Kanter, 1983), little empirical research exists on how issues become initiatives and how initiatives evolve into emergent routines.

For an issue to become an initiative, it must be associated with a course of action and supported by a group of people. Existing case studies and research (Burgelman, 1983b; Hutt, Reingen, & Ronchetto, 1988; Kanter, 1983) suggest that the process involves cultivating social networks (Bower, 1970; Kanter, 1983) and highlights the importance of one-on-one exchanges during this early phase. The initiator is likely to "tin cup" (Kanter, 1983), garnering favors from others using past favors, personal relationships, or reputations as currency. The central figure in renewal now becomes the individual who is associated with the strategic issue rather than the idea generator. Since much of the knowledge surrounding the initiative is still implicit and underdeveloped, participation is based more on bargaining, individual credibility, and interpersonal trust. The *quality* of the idea behind the initiative—still not even fully developed—often becomes secondary.

At this point, then, the need for strong social ties becomes apparent (Burt, 1992a). An individual's ability to get others to change their behavior, offer new forms of cooperation, and put resources at risk is likely to depend on their friendship network (Krackhardt, 1992) and the presence of mutual trust in these relationships (Deutsch, 1958). The specific kinds of trust required to make cooperation possible and to facilitate organizationally risky investments are based on how well members of a network know each other (knowledge-based trust) and on the existence of common desires and motives (identification-based trust; Lewicki & Bunker, 1996). Knowledge-based trust increases predictability and reduces subjective risk, while identification-based trust increases the likelihood that the members see their interests as congruent. The number and quality of such trusting relationships depend, in turn, on the perception that the central figure is competent, open, concerned, and reliable (Butler & Cantrell, 1984; Hosmer, 1995; Mishra, 1996).

It is important to note that strong ties that are the product of formal organization relationships are unlikely to be sufficient in this context. By definition, emergent initiatives require new relationships and novel combinations of resources that are not contemplated in the existing strategy. Thus, at the network level, "strong-form trustworthiness"— when formal governance plays little or no role in the willingness to trust (Barney & Hansen, 1994)—may be important to strategic renewal.

> *P8:* Cooperation within the emergent social network is based on strong informal social ties and high levels of interpersonal trust.

Figure 6.4 illustrates the emergent social network associated with initiatives at the earliest stage of their development. The network is hierarchical, made up of a central figure (the initiator) involved in one-on-one exchanges with several others. Each of the outer nodes in the figure acts independently of the others, providing some sort of direct support to the initiative's development. It is important to note that who participates in this process is based on the resource needs of the initiative, and though these may be accessible through friendship networks, they may also require the initiator to develop new social relationships. Formerly weak or nonexistent social ties may develop into stronger, recurrent relationships.

In a toy manufacturing company we studied, for example, a product manager was struggling to get a pilot project off the ground. In the process, he solicited tiny but crucial amounts of resources from individu-

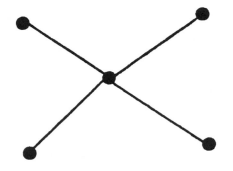

Figure 6.4. An Example of a Hierarchical Emergent Social Network

als in the engineering and production functions with whom he had limited previous interaction. Part of culling the necessary favors involved building these relationships, and much of this was done informally during drinks and conversation at a local tavern. Over time, new friendships and a common understanding of the initiative emerged; by the end of the pilot, the product manager had become the center of a new social network.

> *P9:*   *Early in the development of an initiative, a hierarchical social network emerges in which the participation of individuals and subgroups is coordinated through a globally central actor.*

As the process continues, the initiator discusses the idea repeatedly with others (Bower, 1970; Burgelman, 1991; Kidder, 1981), and as a result of this articulation process, the subjective knowledge associated with the idea becomes increasingly explicit (Nonaka, 1994). The core idea is further refined and developed through these exchanges. Keywords and phrases representing the budding initiative begin to emerge. As the central figure in this process, the initiator accumulates the knowledge from these separate discussions, codifying it into an explicit rationale that gives the initiative a certain strategic logic. This can then be shared with increasing numbers of individuals of disparate functional backgrounds and at different hierarchical levels, and the emergent network begins to expand across the organization. From a knowledge perspective, then, a significant outcome is the creation of explicit, group-level knowledge (i.e., a common language; Spender, 1996) concerning the initiative's underlying logic and strategic relevance. What starts as a purely subjective idea, therefore, begins to develop an intersubjective character, and this lays important groundwork for the initiative's viability at future stages in the process.

> P10: *Articulation of the issue within the emerging network creates explicit, group-level belief concerning the initiative's substance, strategic relevance, and underlying logic.*

Elaboration and the Development of Emergent Routines

In addition, there is a second important type of group knowledge created during this stage. As various functional areas begin to support an initiative, their existing functional-level, *procedural* knowledge begins to be reconsidered (Kogut & Zander, 1992). In support of an experimental project, a purchasing department, for example, might identify and learn to work with a new class of vendors. Similarly, the marketing area might learn how to work within a new distribution channel. To the extent these activities go beyond "mind experiments," they become tangible manifestations of what the idea means for organizational reality. Put differently, they become trial runs, pilot projects, and other types of organized experiments. When successful, experimentation contributes to the success of the idea in passing a new, more rigorous set of epistemological criteria. Organizations rarely accept subjective intuitions, or truths believed by only one individual (unless, of course, the individual happens to be a member of the upper echelon). Instead, they impose an empiricist's logic, requiring that an idea prove itself in terms that suit numerous functional perspectives.

Later on, once there is sufficient explicit knowledge concerning the strategic logic of the initiative, the initiator may become less central and the social network emerging around the initiative may become less hierarchical. At this stage, knowledge about the initiative can be transferred among various participants who now share a common logic. Rather than working through a central figure, then, contributing subunits may now begin to interact directly, working together in new ways and learning from these new experiences. Thus, new social interaction patterns continue to emerge as the social network developing around the initiative evolves from that shown in Figure 6.4 to resemble those shown in Figure 6.5.

Figure 6.5. Evolving Social Networks Over the Course of an Initiative's Development

The nodes in Figure 6.5 may be thought of as individual actors representing various subunits. Considered this way, every node depicted is relatively central to the initiative's development. At the outset, the initiator is the most "globally" central actor in that he or she represents the point where various subefforts come together. The individual actors representing their respective subunits are "locally" central in that they link their subunits to others. Again, although these individuals may not always be identified officially as middle managers,[2] their role as linking pins between subunits makes them middle managers in the functional sense of the term used here.

> *P11:*   *Later in the development of an initiative, codification of the*
> *knowledge related to an initiative reduces reliance on a globally*
> *central actor and increases self-coordination among locally central*
> *actors.*

The specifics of how social networks evolve around the development of an initiative, then, depend to a great degree on the knowledge and skills of individual actors as well as on friendship networks and interpersonal trust. More specifically, there seem to be two categories of knowledge and skills likely to influence which middle managers become central in the development of an initiative. First, since feasible initiatives draw from existing knowledge within the organization, actors with individual-level knowledge—both explicit and implicit, that is, connected closely with the existing core capabilities of the organization—will likely become central to the process. These actors will be central in the reconfiguration of knowledge within a functional area or specialty. Second, those actors with unique resources (e.g., contacts, reputations, interpersonal skills) that can advance linkages across key subgroups may also become central. These actors are important to the development and reconfiguration of the procedural knowledge associated with the coordination of work *across* subgroups.

The patterns shown in Figure 6.5 constitute an evolving form of new procedural knowledge. As the development of the initiative continues, established routines that coordinate work across subunits are modified. Stated differently, the existing procedural knowledge that allows subunits to work together is reconfigured and new organizational routines are created. In the process, knowledge is transformed once again by social interaction (Nonaka, 1994). This time, the explicit, group-level knowledge that had been the substance of communication exchanges in the network is further transformed into the implicit, group-level knowledge associated with changing organization routines.

> P12: *Interactions among subunits reconfigure existing functional knowledge and alter the patterns of coordination between subgroups, leading to the development of procedural knowledge in the form of emergent organizational routines.*

It is important to note, however, that because the initiative has not been endorsed by top management, at this point, the scope of new activity is limited and experimental. Thus, the knowledge associated with the original idea has grown significantly, but it is still incomplete and tangential to core capability.

Ratification: Linking Initiatives to Official Strategy

To complete the cycle of strategic renewal, emergent routines must become part of the organization's repertoire of operating routines—its organizational capability base. This process follows a pragmatic logic. First, emergent initiatives are somehow linked in cause-effect fashion to the organization's overarching purpose. This and practical self-interest motivate actors at the top of the organization to change their personal beliefs about the definition of organizational success and the substance of official strategy. As renewal proceeds, the result is formal commitment of resources and sanction for emergent routines. By fueling the growth, reconfiguration, and formalization of social networks, the ratification of an emergent strategic initiative by top management begins the process of integration, whereby systems, structures, norms, and values are reconfigured to support a renewed set of core capabilities (Leonard-Barton, 1992; Walsh & Ungson, 1991).

Emergent initiatives do not suddenly become acceptable alternative strategies. By the time initiatives gain top managers' attention, much of the strategic logic (i.e., the connection between the initiative and organizational goals) has already been developed at functional and subunit levels. In addition, the cognitive context in which top managers become aware of an initiative is influenced by middle-level managers' ongoing attempts to direct their attention to and understand the strategic issues facing the firm (Dutton & Ashford, 1993; Floyd & Wooldridge, 1996). Often, for example, middle-level managers' ability to link an initiative to the competitive threats or opportunities facing the organization (Dutton & Jackson, 1987) is key to integrating formerly divergent beliefs into the executive mind-set. In this way, a subtle and gradual change occurs in the socially constructed definition of official strategy.

> P13: Issue selling by middle managers provides a stimulus that motivates
> top managers to begin to change their definition of strategy.

Paralleling this mental shift, objective circumstances frequently contribute to the acceptance of divergent proposals. In his analysis of the bottom-up process that led to Intel's exit from the memory business and transformation into a "microprocessor company," Burgelman (1994) notes that the proposals for investing in microprocessor capacity were funded with little a priori awareness of their implications for official strategy. The use of objectively based arguments by middle-level champions in an atmosphere of "constructive confrontation" allowed microprocessor projects to succeed because they responded more appropriately to customer demand. This occurred despite the fact that senior managers were vocal in their disagreement with the idea of exiting the "core business" (i.e., memory chips).

P14:   Objectively based appeals demonstrating responsiveness to specific
       issues allow initiatives to survive despite their inconsistency with
       official strategy.

The Intel case, however, illustrates not only how a divergent initiative
can grow despite its incompatibility with official strategy, but also how
an initiative can supplant existing strategy. In the end, the top management of Intel was faced with overwhelming evidence that an aggressive
pursuit of the microprocessor business constituted a qualitatively
better strategy than remaining in the memory business.

The cycle of strategic renewal comes full circle, then, when top managers recognize that the goal behind a divergent initiative contributes
not to the current strategy but to a superior strategy. It is then that the
cognitive foundation has been established for integrating the initiative
into the organizational mainstream. In this context, "better" is evalu-
ated in highly subjective terms, such as "more profitable," "more responsible," "more responsive," and so on, and the nature of these subjective criteria depends on the higher-order values held by top
management. In other words, for top managers to give up their notion
of "who we are" or "what business we are in," links to higher-order purposes are a necessary part of the process.

Nonaka (1994) shares with Quinn (1980) the view that top managers
play a directive role, even in bottom-up, middle-up-down, or (in
Quinn's terms) incremental processes. For Nonaka, commitments to
(the ratification of) initiatives result from their fit with top managers'
future vision of what "ought to be." The vision, however, is often very
abstract, "linking seemingly disparate activities or businesses into a coherent whole" (Nonaka, 1994, p. 31). We have all heard universal conceptualizations of organizational intention, such as "We bring good
things to life," "[We are] the Document company," or "We are in the
hospitality business."

This kind of top management vision, though it may be critical, provides little substantive guidance in the generation of specific initiatives.
Moreover, the values component of the vision may have little to do with
the capability-specific values identified in Leonard-Barton's (1992)
analysis of core capabilities. Instead, the vision includes such universal
values as integrity, respect for people, beauty, and so on. The kind of vision from middle managers that is relevant to the creation of new
knowledge and the renewal of capability is often similarly equivocal

and may similarly articulate important values. These visions can be the bridge for initiatives that diverge from official strategy.

> P15:   *Ratification is associated with the recognition by top management*
> *that an emergent strategic initiative represents a qualitatively better*
> *strategy as defined by its compatibility with high-order*
> *organization values.*

The Politics of Ratification

In addition to its teleological dimension, the process of ratification contains a political element. To ratify a divergent initiative, top managers, or at least one top manager, must come to see the proposal as consistent with their own self-interest. This minimum political threshold, required for the deployment of significant resources, has been identified directly and indirectly in much of the strategy literature (Andrews, 1971; Bower, 1970; Bower & Doz, 1979; Eisenhardt & Zbaracki, 1992; Johnson, 1987; Lindblom, 1959; Narayanan & Fahey, 1982; Pettigrew, 1973). Concern with self-interest, of course, is hardly limited to top management. As already noted, middle- and operating-level managers must buy into (i.e., commit to and support) an initiative. And although our model has not emphasized the fact that politics is involved in earlier stages of initiative development, there is evidence to support its existence throughout the process of strategic renewal (Bower, 1970; Burgelman, 1983c; Kanter, 1983).

At the ratification stage, however, the political side of renewal becomes especially salient. It is at this point in the process that organization members increasingly ask questions such as, Do we really want to adopt this new way of doing things and give up other activities? Is this initiative good for the organization as a whole or just good for the group that supports it? Should we reconsider our agreed-upon goals and strategy? What will this change mean for my status in the organization? On a smaller scale, these essentially political questions may be raised in the process of developing the initiative into an emergent routine. When the proposal reaches top management, however, the stakes are raised significantly. What has been a rather small-scale activity takes on the potential of affecting the whole organization. This new reality stimulates political activity as individuals lobby to influence others, form alliances, and in numerous other ways stake their positions (Narayanan & Fahey, 1982).

> P16: *Political activity reaches its zenith as the renewal process approaches ratification.*

Ultimately, however, for an initiative to achieve ratification, those supporting it must emerge from the fray of political activity to persuade influential others, notably top managers. Developing an ally in the top team early in the process is one way successful coalitions gain such influence. Participation by a senior manager in the emerging social network can help steer the initiative in ways that avoid potential analytical and political pitfalls. Bower (1970), for example, provides several cases of top managers who vouch for the credibility of initiatives coming from below.

> P17: *Ratification is facilitated when a member of top management participates in the emergent social network associated with an initiative.*

Even short of eliciting their full participation, however, having contact with those at the top may help middle-level champions internalize information on the informal rules governing top management decisions. Typically, rule by formal authority is accompanied by informal rules, such as norms about what types of initiatives are supported by which senior executives. Formally, rules are often rational, involving comprehensive analysis of costs and future returns and comprehensive means-ends assessments of how the proposal integrates with the strategic aims of the organization (Fredrickson, 1984). Informally, however, influence may be distributed unevenly among the top management group, depending on the nature of the decision in question. In many cases, the chief executive and a few select members of the group may represent a dominant coalition whose support is required for virtually any strategic decision (Pettigrew, 1992).

Informal norms are highly idiosyncratic to the organization, but knowing them may be critical to smoothing the way for strategic initiatives (Bower, 1970). Identifying supporters early while avoiding exposure to powerful opponents can be key in building political momentum in advance of formal authorization. By the time the initiative comes up for formal ratification, such momentum may carry an initiative that otherwise would be "shot down" by a vocal enemy at the top. Because they are implicit, however, knowledge of these informal rules may not be widely disseminated within the organization. Navigating a process that is ostensibly rational yet also political is a complex task, and in part, the inability of middle-level actors to comprehend top team dynamics may explain why many renewal efforts fail at this stage. Indeed, keen political awareness is a distinctive marker of successful organizational champions (Burgelman, 1983c; Floyd & Wooldridge, 1996).

> P18: Ratification of emergent initiatives is facilitated when those championing the initiative possess an awareness of the informal norms governing top management decisions.

In addition to having an appreciation for decision norms, it may also be important for managers championing proposals to gauge the timing of their upward influence efforts. Research has shown that the level of convergence among top management on a particular strategy is related to the strategy's "age" (Johnson, 1988) and that, at later stages of a strategy's development, the level of commitment to the status quo may be quite high. From the perspective of a middle-level champion, a tightly knit top management team (TMT) that strongly agrees on a particular strategic direction may represent a barrier to the ratification of divergent alternatives. For the organization, this may have serious consequences for strategic renewal and the development of new capabilities.

> P19: High levels of consensus toward official strategy among the TMT may impede the ratification of an emergent strategic initiative.

More broadly, there is no clear evidence that a high level of agreement among members of top management is desirable from any perspective. Studies of top management consensus (Bourgeois, 1980; Dess, 1987; Dess & Origer, 1987) have shown no consistent relationship between consensus and organizational performance (Wooldridge & Floyd, 1989). In one study, however, an interesting relationship was uncovered between the level of consensus on the environment and the *in*accuracy of environmental perceptions within the TMT (Bourgeois, 1980). This is consistent with the notion that too much consensus too early in a decision-making process leads to poor-quality strategic decisions (Schweiger, Sandberg, & Rechner, 1989). More generally, one can see high levels of TMT consensus toward strategy as a form of strategic inertia (Huff et al., 1992).

However, although TMT consensus may increase with the passage of time, it is also true that strategies tend to become out of sync with environmental conditions over time and that increasing "strategic drift" (Johnson, 1988) may create sufficient stress (Huff et al., 1992) in the organization to motivate reconsideration of the strategic direction. Signs of stress include poor financial results, dissatisfaction among stakeholders or organizational actors, technological advances by competitors, and so on. As a result of stress, the level of consensus within the top team may begin to deteriorate, and this creates a decision-making atmosphere that is more conducive to emergent initiatives.

> P20: The ratification of emergent strategic initiatives may be facilitated when indicators of strategic drift and stress are associated with official strategy.

From Divergent Proposals to Organizational Routines

Once a proposal has been ratified by top management, the responsibility for integrating emergent networks and routines into the organizational structure and capability base typically falls on middle-level actors (Schendel & Hofer, 1979). As mentioned in Chapters 1 and 2, there is a fairly diverse body of literature on the tactics middle managers use to carry out top management's decisions (Hrebiniak & Joyce, 1984; Nutt, 1987). Although insightful on the question of how initiatives are transformed into routines, this research is less salient to the question of how initiatives become integrated into the established capabilities of the organization. Here the key question is how are new capabilities retained in light of existing capabilities? Put differently, how do organizations avoid contaminating present decisions and new routines with the systems, knowledge, and values of past decisions and old routines?

Walsh and Ungson's (1991) theory of organizational memory offers a number of useful suggestions. As noted in Chapter 4, they identify the facilities for retaining organizational knowledge as including individuals, transformations, structures, ecology, and culture. Transformations, structures, and physical ecology capture the routines, relationships, and procedures associated with capability, but only individuals and culture retain both the stimulus for a decision and the organizational response. When a decision is made to ratify a divergent strategic initiative and change official strategy, the collective memory is called on to determine which of the existing routines, if any, are to be abandoned and/or which of the existing routines, if any, are to be modified or elaborated to support the new strategic direction. This requires a collective memory that connects decision stimuli to potential responses and hence draws on organizational culture—that is, the organization's shared beliefs "about the who, what, when, where and how of a decision stimulus and response" (Walsh & Ungson, 1991, p. 68). In short, an organization's ability to integrate new routines into the existing capability base depends on its collective memory of past decision stimuli and responses (i.e., the existence of a shared ideology).

> P21: A shared belief system facilitates the integration of new routines
>   into the existing capability base.

The evolution of shared beliefs or culture, in turn, depends on the pattern of social interactions within the group, including its communication patterns, authority relationships, and friendship networks (Weick, 1995). Because of their unique position in the hierarchy, middle-level actors are likely to retain information about the connections between stimulus and response. In fact, the stimulus-response terminology can be seen as a more general way to describe the relationship between strategy and operations. As we argued in Chapter 3, it is middle-level managers who are exposed to both the details of how to get things done (i.e., who can do what) and the strategic logic about when and where specific kinds of actions are appropriate. Thus, the process of changing or abandoning existing capabilities and integrating new ones activates the knowledge base of middle-level actors.

> P22: Knowledge about the connection between decision stimulus and
>   organizational response will be concentrated in the middle levels of
>   the organization hierarchy.

In most cases, the cohort of middle-level actors involved in the integration subprocess will be far larger than the initiating coalition. In addition, members of the integrating cohort may oppose the initiative because they see it as inconsistent with either the organization's interest, their subunit's interest, or their personal self-interest (Guth & MacMillan, 1986; Wooldridge & Floyd, 1989). In some instances, new routines may require the abandonment of functional activities directed by a middle manager. Whether new routines are successfully integrated therefore depends not only on knowledge that tends to be concentrated at middle levels but also on how middle-level organization members perceive the tradeoff between organizational change and self-interest. In short, integration depends on the commitments that middle managers are willing to make, and these are dependent on whether they foresee the outcomes of the change process as fair. How, then, can their perceptions of equity be maintained in the face of the potential challenges to self-interest posed by strategic renewal?

> P23: *Commitment toward divergent strategic initiatives is related to how change affects members' perceptions of equity.*

To some degree, it may be possible to create incentives that encourage people to change. Economic incentives, such as "golden parachutes" (Buchholz & Ribbens, 1994), are common for top managers as a means to encourage them to accept changes in strategy that threaten their self-interests. Incentives for risk taking and intrapreneurship are also frequently advocated for people at middle levels of the hierarchy (e.g., Floyd & Wooldridge, 1996; Kanter, 1982). To be seen as equitable, however, the connection between contribution (performance) and outcome (reward) must be understood and accepted (Adams, 1963). This creates a problem with the use of bureaucratic rewards in strategic renewal because it implies prior, explicit articulation of behaviors that may be divergent and inconsistent with official goals. Offering explicit rewards for such behavior may undermine efficiency, and though a certain amount of "chaos" may be useful in organizations (Stacey, 1995), reliance on bureaucratic systems alone to stimulate divergent behavior may have unanticipated, dysfunctional consequences.

> P24: *Bureaucratic rewards will be insufficient to foster acceptance of divergent strategic initiatives.*

Renewal occurs in an environment where the definition of performance is in a state of flux. Old routines are changing, and the definition of contribution for certain individuals and groups is likely to be highly equivocal. In such an ambiguous context, clan controls (Ouichi, 1980; Wilkins & Ouichi, 1983) may induce members to believe that they will be treated fairly, despite the unknown consequences for their self-interests. A clan is a group of people whose interactions are based on mutual trust and whose members are socialized to value common goals (Ouichi, 1980). The sense that they are bound together and share a common future is heartened by the belief that they will be treated equitably. Consistent with complexity theory, clan controls may represent a form of "semistructures" (Brown & Eisenhardt, 1997) that facilitate coherent patterns of social interaction (existing routines), on the one hand, and yet cultivate new ways of doing things (new routines), on the other.

> P25:   *The existence of clan controls may help to increase commitment*
>   *toward a divergent strategic initiative.*

Once the relationship between the ratification decision and organizational response becomes clear and members commit to adopting new routines, the challenge of integration involves a process of diffusing new knowledge throughout the organization. Again, because we are describing shifts in core capabilities, the scope of the knowledge transfer problem is likely to be quite large, reaching across many functions and subunits. As noted, the process of developing the initiative involves articulating tacit knowledge as well as learning new procedural skills, and realizing new core capabilities requires a similar diffusion process in the broader venue. Accordingly, the organizational learning required by integration will be facilitated by the use of rich information-processing mechanisms (Daft & Lengel, 1986; Egelhoff, 1988; Galbraith, 1977) such as apprenticeship and observation, as well as the codification and communication of new routines in the form of action plans, formal training, standard operating procedures, new organization charts, and so forth. Although richer mechanisms such as personnel transfers, experiential learning modalities, and other forms of tacit knowledge diffusion are costly and time-consuming, they may be essential to the process of renewing core capabilities. As noted in Chapter 4, as a source of sustained advantage, core capabilities rely significantly on tacit knowledge (Kogut & Zander, 1993; Nonaka, 1994), and the ability to transfer tacit knowledge may therefore constitute a further deterrence to imitation (Teece et al., 1997).

> **P26:** *The diffusion of new routines will be facilitated by the use of rich information-processing mechanisms such as apprenticeship, observation, and personnel transfer.*

Discussion

The emphasis on culture, clan controls, and rich information-processing mechanisms in our description of the integration process differs significantly from more traditional descriptions of strategy implementation. Typically, these involve more or less linear transformations of strategy concepts into new structures, systems, and people and rely on a static, means-end form of reasoning. Our description of integration, however, relies on a complex, adaptive logic. The difference is not purely semantic. Fundamentally, renewal is an emergent, generative process (Hart, 1992). Rather than deducing appropriate action from strategic premises, therefore, integration follows an inductive logic—it begins with action and experience, and the pattern of interactions is knowable only after the fact.

This approach to understanding organizational change relies not so much on the idea that reality is socially constructed but on the idea that what people *think* about reality is socially constructed. Put differently, the process of integration is a "sense-making" process (Weick, 1995). Ratification of a new initiative by powerful top managers gets people's attention. It interrupts their routine ways of behaving and requires them to do things differently. With the emergence of new behaviors, organization members, from the CEO down to the operating-level employee, begin to construct new mental frameworks to make sense, retrospectively, of how things have changed. These new mental frameworks and the new social interactions that accompany them become part of the knowledge base and routines that make up capability. They quickly begin to govern how people perceive reality and what they pay attention to. They affect the interpretation of events and once again may prevent members from accepting divergent ideas or perceiving the need for change.

Thus, the integration process brings us full circle to the question of how organizations generate new ideas in the face of a dominant logic. The fact that renewal is an emergent process and follows an inductive logic does not avoid the cognitive and social rigidities often associated with strategic decision making. Indeed, theory suggests that capability development is highly path dependent (Dierickx & Cool, 1989; Teece et al., 1997). Still, the fact that it relies on change in members' mental models and in intersubjectively shared meanings does not mean that renewal is necessarily unnatural or difficult. As we have argued, under the right set of conditions, organizations may become complex adaptive systems for which change is cardinal.

In Chapter 7, as part of our discussion of high-priority research issues, we consider conditions likely to support strategic renewal. Before closing this chapter, however, it is important to clarify our position concerning the role of top managers in strategic renewal. In taking a middle-level perspective, we are not asserting that top managers are not important to renewal, only that their role is different. Consider Quinn's (1980) depiction of top managers, for example. In his model of logical incrementalism, senior managers (and particularly the chief executive) behave as cagey manipulators, planting the seeds of an idea among subordinates and encouraging particular individuals to act as organizational champions. The "logic" of what appears to be a political process lies in the rationality of delaying overt commitment and surfacing additional information. This reduces both the political and business uncertainties associated with the initiative. Top managers are given credit for perceiving the need for change and shaping the sociology of the organization to achieve it.

The nature of change described by Quinn, however, may not be as radical as that contemplated in strategic renewal. In particular, it is difficult—though not impossible—to imagine a chief executive encouraging initiatives that challenge his or her vision, personal beliefs, or value system. To the extent these are represented in current strategic priorities, top managers are unlikely to stimulate divergent initiatives directly. Thus, we would argue that, in most cases, top managers provide a stimulus to renewal not by direct influence but by creating the organizational arrangements (Burgelman, 1994) and cultural norms associated with tolerance for divergent points of view. Many organizations, for example, have adopted the use of developmental projects as a device for stimulating new capabilities (Leonard-Barton, 1992). In sum, the middle-level perspective adopted here holds that top managers are critical in the creation of the context in which strategic renewal occurs. In addition, top managers are also participants in the social learning process that underlies strategy formation.

Notes

1. Stacey notes Krackhardt's (1992) "contradictory" argument that strong ties increase members' feelings of security, make them more willing to change, and therefore lead to more variety in behavior. In our view, Granovetter's and Krackhardt's positions are compatible. As discussed below, strong ties are important later in the initiative development process, at the point where informal networks begin to emerge around a central actor.

2. They could be operating-level managers or managers of staff departments, for example.

7 Research Approaches and Future Directions

> We need more insight into how new ideas are generated.... We need a much greater understanding of how and why midlevel leaders emerge.... We need to learn more about the ratification and integration process.

In this final chapter, we take a look at the research questions and methodologies that seem most relevant to a middle-level perspective of strategy. As a way to organize the discussion, Figure 7.1 highlights three focal points, or categories of research. The first category concerns research on the strategic renewal process itself. Although Chapter 6 is an attempt to develop a model identifying and highlighting relationships among important elements of the process, the model must be considered underspecified. Thus, it is critical that future work continue to build the field's understanding of the renewal process. To avoid building "castles in the sky," however, theory-testing research should remain important as a way to keep pace with new theory development.

The second category of research noted in the figure examines relationships between intraorganizational conditions and strategic renewal. By describing strategic renewal as a complex adaptive system, Chapter 6 made numerous assumptions concerning salient organizational antecedents and arrangements. While existing thinking in the organizational sciences offers clues regarding antecedents of renewal, empirical studies examining critical relationships are needed.

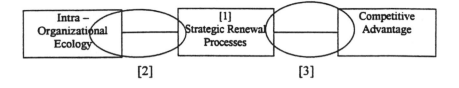

Figure 7.1. Three Focal Points for Researching Renewal From a Midlevel Perspective

The third category focuses on competitive advantage: If strategic renewal driven from the middle is to become a prominent focus in strategic management research, it must ultimately be linked to sustained competitive advantage and organizational performance. Again, existing theory suggests strong arguments for the link between process and performance, but empirical research should examine the strength and nature of this relationship. Overall, we look for further evidence of the role played by actors in the middle of the organization in all three research agendas.

We now consider each of these categories of research in more detail. To organize our discussion, each section begins by considering the state of existing theory. Following this, we describe what we believe to be the most relevant high-priority research issues. Finally, we end each section with a discussion of appropriate methodologies and, where appropriate, exemplary research.

The Midlevel Strategic Renewal Process Theory

The model of strategic renewal presented in the previous chapter was developed from a synthesis of existing case studies and relevant theory. Many of the linkages in the model are logical deductions, and while we hope they have a ring of truth, in its current stage of development, the framework is untested. We do not really know, for example, the degree to which weak ties are important in the idea generation process. We also cannot say with certainty how social networks emerge around the development of a new initiative. Obviously, then, empirical research is needed to examine the constructs and relationships described in the model.

More fundamentally, however, it seems unlikely that the model has, at this stage, specified all of the relevant constructs and linkages. In other words, the model is incomplete and more work needs to be done specifying the mechanisms that underlie strategic renewal in large organizations. Theory-building research in this area therefore continues to be important.

High-Priority Research Issues

A basic argument of this book is that the strategy field needs to further advance its basic understanding of the strategic renewal process. In our view, research should continue to produce studies that provide fine-grained descriptions of how strategic renewal takes place in specific settings. Case studies, using both qualitative and quantitative methods, seem especially important in this area. Book-length exemplars include Bower's (1970) early book, Johnson's (1987) later study, and Pettigrew's (1985) account of Imperial Chemical Industries PLC. Each of these longer treatments permits detailed clinical and theoretical analysis not possible in most journal-length articles.

But what questions should guide researchers in developing case studies? First, we need more insight into how new ideas are generated. The theory reviewed here suggests the importance of subjective beliefs and novel social relationships. It can probably be said, however, that all individuals hold subjective beliefs and most likely have some unexpected or unique social contacts. The present framework does little to explain why new ideas abound in some organizations and are relatively scarce in others.

Second, we need a much greater understanding of how and why midlevel leaders emerge. Perhaps most important, the present framework assumes that midlevel actors take on leadership roles and relinquish them more or less automatically as conditions warrant. Indeed, our own research (Floyd & Wooldridge, 1997) suggests that, in high-performing firms, different managers influence the strategic renewal process at different points in time. But how does this occur? What keeps an emergent social structure, where one individual has become the central leader, from rigidifying? How much do these processes vary from organization to organization, and why?

Finally, we need to learn more about the ratification and integration process. Top management's ratification of divergent initiatives and their integration into the overall strategy are necessary for completion of the renewal cycle. These activities, however, seem riddled with pitfalls that might stifle future renewal efforts. Ratification, for example, is really only half the story. In evolutionary terms, top managers play an important variation reduction role, and questions remain about how current initiatives can be rejected without discouraging the renewal process over the longer run. On the flip side, ratification and integration "sow the seeds" of rigidity. How does the ratification and integration of one initiative affect others? Do ratification and integration place a temporal hold on other divergent activities?

Research Approaches and Exemplars

The questions discussed above may be usefully examined through a variety of theory-building, as well as theory-testing, approaches. Certainly, the inductive theory-building work of Bower (1970), Kanter (1982, 1983), Mintzberg and McHugh (1985), Pettigrew (1973), Johnson (1988), and, most important, Burgelman (1983c, 1991, 1994) has made an important imprint on the development of the field's knowledge about these issues. Similarly, Westley (1990), Kidder (1981), Leonard-Barton (1992), and Quinn (1980) have derived theory from clinical data using somewhat less formal approaches. All of this work is notable for the significance of its contribution.

Clearly, therefore, inductive theory building represents an important alternative for examining the renewal process. Empirically, this form of work generally involves the development of descriptive cases that are then qualitatively assessed for their implications to existing theory. Since several excellent references on qualitative research exist (see, e.g., Denzin & Lincoln, 1994; Marshall & Rossman, 1989; Miles & Huberman, 1994; Yin, 1995), we will not attempt an in-depth treatment of the topic here. Still, a few key points concerning the use of qualitative methods as they pertain to the middle-level perspective deserve mention.

First, in designing strategy process studies, researchers should consider adopting the "strategic initiative" as the primary unit of analysis (Burgelman, 1991). In doing so, researchers can focus their efforts around "telling the story" behind the development of a particular initiative. This approach has the advantage of focusing attention on a particular event in the firm's history and of providing relatively clear beginning and end points. In addition, the use of this approach creates the possibility that a single organization can provide the setting for multiple, comparative case studies (Yin, 1995). A drawback, of course, is that this approach may give too little attention to the way in which an initiative affects others. More ambitious empirical work therefore would follow the course of a portfolio of issues over time.

Second, researchers should appreciate the context-specific and longitudinal nature of the phenomenon being studied. As described here, renewal is a complex organizational process occurring over a significant period of time. Studies, therefore, should trace the coevolution of individual elements, tying them together into a holistic description of how the process unfolds within particular settings.

Third, researchers conducting qualitative strategy process studies should anticipate the large amount of information that must be managed. Though often overwhelming, the huge data sets typically generated in qualitative studies are necessary not only to understanding but to confirming and verifying emerging conclusions. Importantly, researchers should remember that the use of a primarily qualitative approach does not preclude the inclusion of quantitative data. Oftentimes, data lend themselves to quantification, and in these situations, researchers should "count the countable" (Lee, 1998).

In fact, in our view, researchers should anticipate combining both qualitative and quantitative data as complements in process studies. Using social network analysis, for example, a researcher might quantitatively describe the structure of social relationships within an organization. With this as a context, the researcher could then draw on more qualitative approaches to gain a "finer grain" understanding of the process itself.

The points above are suggestive of the significant challenges posed by case study research. In contrast to more quantitatively based research, case studies are relatively open-ended, and few "road maps" exist. "Like much of the qualitative research domain, there are no hard and fast rules for case study research" (Lee, 1998, p. 121). Researchers become intensely immersed in their studies, often for long periods of time and often with little sense of where things are heading. Far less sequential than quantitative work, qualitative studies often iterate back and forth between data analysis and data collection. Thus, researchers must remain open-minded, flexible, and responsive, as emergent themes must be checked and rechecked against the "reality" of multiple data sources.

Although qualitative research can be seen as somewhat of an art form, where researchers play with emergent ideas, when it is done right, it is also scientific and methodical. The best studies demonstrate rigor through careful documentation and systematic procedures (see, e.g., Eisenhardt & Bourgeois, 1988). Multiple data-collection techniques— such as observation, interviewing, and archival approaches—are often used within a single study (Miles & Huberman, 1994). These multiple data sources not only add insight but also credibility by allowing for comparisons and verification. Regardless of how rigorous the effort is, however, the "acid test" of a qualitative study is whether or not it reveals a good story that has the "ring of truth" and provides new and interesting insights. For interested readers, Eisenhardt (1989) and Yin (1995) provide excellent summaries of the methodological issues in the use of case studies for theory-building purposes. For a discussion of the problems in publishing such research, we recommend the articles in Frost's (1995) volume.

A second approach to the development of new theory is to use logic and prior research as a basis for developing generalizable research propositions. Deductive work of this kind does not necessarily ignore data altogether. Instead, it proceeds based on the conclusions of prior research (Bacharach, 1989) and may even involve the reuse of primary clinical data (Burgelman, 1983b). The strength of this approach is that it synthesizes existing work. It can define new constructs and relationships that are firmly rooted in the current body of knowledge. In addition, deductive work is often useful in resolving inconsistencies in research findings (e.g., Wooldridge & Floyd, 1989). This, then, lays the foundation for more cumulative empirical work.

Jane Dutton and Susan Ashford's (1993) deductive work on issue selling by middle managers illustrates how existing theory can be productively refocused on issues relevant to the middle-level perspective. This work springs from an interest in how top managers allocate their attention to strategic issues and the effects of this process on organizational change (Dutton & Duncan, 1987; Dutton, Fahey, & Narayanan, 1983). The authors apply reasoning from social problem theory, impression management, and upward influence to develop an integrative model of the issue-selling process. On the basis of this rich theoretical grounding, they deduce 22 research propositions, ranging from defining issue-selling success to identifying the dimensions of the process. Although the productivity of a theory cannot be measured in terms of the number of propositions it generates, the holistic description offered in this article provides a solid foundation for empirical work. And these authors have not neglected the obligation to test their own theory. With others, they have recently published empirical work on issue selling by middle managers (Dutton, Ashford, O'Neill, Hayes, & Wierba, 1997).

Indeed, without testing, the usefulness of new theories is limited, particularly if the ultimate goal is a practical one, such as helping managers renew their organization's strategies. For the sake of emphasizing this point, it is worth noting that much of the time the follow-up to theory building never emerges in organizational research. Consider, for example, how few of Mintzberg's or Burgelman's ideas have been subjected to rigorous testing. One of the reasons may be an academic's inclination to make his or her own mark. But the desire to invent new constructs and develop new models has contributed to a "weed patch ... [of] measures, terms, concepts, and research paradigms" in organizational research in general (Pfeffer, 1993, p. 616) and, more specifically, to a "confusing array" of theories in strategy process research (Hart, 1992). Thus, while ambition is admirable, there are many ways to make a contribution, and theory testing may be particularly appropriate for those who are new to a field. Plowing in fields that have been cleared by others has the benefit of enriching one's understanding of the phenomena. The result of this enhanced understanding may be an inspiration for further theory development (Dubin, 1976).

Relationships Between Organizational
Conditions and Strategic Renewal

Theory

Our assumption that new capabilities emerge from socially complex processes suggests that strategic renewal does not depend on a simple set of antecedent conditions. Yet here we identify organizational conditions that seem necessary for renewal to occur. The contradiction is apparent rather than real. Our reference to antecedent conditions is not

Table 7.1   Important Antecedents of Midlevel Strategic Renewal

---

Strategic Knowledge

Strategic Priorities
Organizational Capabilities
Strategic Context
Strategic Consensus

Strategic Motivation

Top Management Expectations
Organizational Commitment
Trust and Perceived Fairness
Organizational Reward Systems

Strategic Autonomy

Top Management Leadership Style
Organizational Structure
Organizational Control Systems
Organizational Culture

---

meant to suggest that these determine how process unfolds. There is no expectation that researchers will be able to make specific predictions about the process (e.g., how new ideas will be generated or initiatives developed) from particular antecedent conditions. Consistent with complexity theory (Waldrop, 1992), the emphasis in this section is on the general conditions that are consistent with ongoing strategic renewal in large, complex organizations.

Drawing from theory presented at various points throughout this book, Table 7.1 summarizes important antecedent conditions into three broad categories. First, a central argument in favor of a middle-level perspective is that strategic knowledge is greatest within the middle of the organization. We have argued that the middle level is where knowledge about direction, operations, and context is most likely to come together to form a complete strategic picture. Our model of adaptive strategic renewal, therefore, is built on the assumption that midlevel actors possess significant strategic knowledge. Second, our model assumes motivation on the part of midlevel actors. Championing, facilitating, and otherwise promoting new strategic initiatives requires leadership on the part of midlevel actors, and the ideas presented here have assumed that individuals are motivated to act strategically. Finally, in describing strategic renewal, we have assumed a significant degree of midlevel autonomy. Renewal requires actors to engage in activities and take chances that go beyond top management intentions. There is an assumption, then, that it is important to study the middle when these organizational members have the autonomy and support to affect change. As we will see in the following section, each of these assumptions is consistent with complexity theory but each raises important issues for further research.

High-Priority Research Issues

The assertion that various forms of strategic knowledge come together in the middle of the organization raises several important research issues. While included here as an antecedent, it should be remembered that strategic knowledge is accumulated and altered throughout the process.

In addition to questions about appropriate *levels* of strategic knowledge within firms, the issue of knowledge raises questions concerning the impact of consensus, or shared understanding, on the process. Existing research assessing the effect of consensus on organizational performance has been limited to consensus among members of the top management team, and it has produced equivocal findings (Bourgeois, 1980; Dess, 1987; Priem, 1990). A midlevel perspective on strategy making, however, suggests the need for studies that broaden the scope of consensus to include a wider variety of organizational actors (Wooldridge & Floyd, 1989).

Traditional arguments in favor of consensus hold that shared thinking promotes integrative behavior. Conversely, the tendency toward "groupthink" (Janis, 1972) is the most prominent argument weighing in against consensus. The view of strategy presented here suggests a slightly different tension: the need for divergent thinking in the generation of new ideas versus the need for cooperative behavior in the development of new initiatives. Again, this issue may relate to the evolution of strategic knowledge and thinking at various stages of the renewal process (Floyd & Wooldridge, 1999; Wooldridge & Floyd, 1989).

As described by Waldrop (1992), complex adaptive systems are made up of "imperfectly smart agents," each pursuing his or her own self-interest. Strategic renewal, therefore, may not require actors to possess perfect strategic knowledge or to think alike. Rather, it may be enough that actors simply broaden their perspectives and think strategically. What types of knowledge, how much consensus on what issues, and at what point in the process, then, become important issues in midlevel strategy process research.

Waldrop's observation is also suggestive of our second category of important antecedents, the need for motivation, or self-interest, on the part of midlevel actors. Although previous research has, at times, viewed midlevel actors as impediments to strategy (Guth & MacMillan, 1986), the present framework is built on the assumption that it is in the individual's self-interest to help the firm achieve and maintain strategic effectiveness. For many firms, however, such an assumption may not be warranted. In American firms especially, middle managers more often than not have been left out of the strategic "conversation" (Westley, 1990). In many cases, they have been viewed as "deadwood," candidates for downsizing. For their part, American managers generally identify more with their professional specialties than with individual firms, and many career professionals change firms regularly as opportunities present themselves. How, then, can strategic renewal emanating from the organization's middle be expected to occur in such an environment?

Indeed, the motivation of individuals to engage in voluntary strategic renewal efforts may be the most important characteristic distinguishing adaptive organizations. But how is this motivation fostered? What is the role of top management leadership in bringing this about? How can formal reward systems be used to encourage nonsanctioned activity? In short, while conditions in many large organizations favor compliant behavior, research should attempt to identify how adaptive firms encourage individuals to act entrepreneurially on behalf of the organization.

Finally, our model of strategic renewal is built on the premise that midlevel actors have the autonomy to bring about strategic change. Like all complex adaptive systems, strategic renewal requires the appropriate balance between top-down order and bottom-up diversity (Holland, 1975). In a recent study, for example, Brown and Eisenhardt (1997) note the prominence of "semi-structures" in organizations that demonstrate continual change. Although students of organization have long recognized the need for "loose-tight" arrangements (e.g., Peters & Waterman, 1980), achieving the appropriate balance continues to be problematic. A critical research issue remains then: What is the appropriate balance, and how do firms achieve and maintain it?

The questions in each research area must be reconsidered in different national settings. Perceptions and the desirability of autonomy and involvement, for example, change from culture to culture. But in our view, there is a tendency to overestimate the effects of cultural differences (Markoczy, 1997). Certainly, manifestations of social relations differ across cultures. We assert, however, that relationships among fundamental social factors (e.g., autonomy, involvement, trust) and renewal are pan-cultural. For researchers, this suggests a need to be sensitive to differences in how various factors reveal themselves. For the management of global organizations, our assertion suggests a need for culturally tailored organizational arrangements.

Appropriate Research Methods

Existing theory can be used to suggest relationships between the constructs included in Table 7.1 and the strategic renewal process. For the most part, therefore, research within this category should be designed to test proposed relationships. Certainly, many of the issues discussed above can be addressed through cross-sectional designs using quantitative measures.

Before turning to the discussion of such research, we must acknowledge that many interesting issues in this category—notably, questions surrounding the evolution of important factors such as knowledge or trust over the course of the process—will also require the use of longitudinal, case-based designs. A study might, for example, begin with the premise that new initiatives are born of divergent and narrowly held strategic beliefs. Through an in-depth case study, the researcher could then examine how knowledge becomes diffused and more widely shared as the initiative develops. Research of this variety has a great potential to make significant contributions to our overall understanding of strategic renewal. Indeed, our own bias is that case studies, designed for theory testing (Yin, 1995), will often allow researchers to address more significant issues and yield richer insights and findings.

Cross-sectional studies have many advantages, however, and are appropriate for examining many relationships that could be generated from Table 7.1. Broadly, we can segment the types of studies needed into two categories: studies examining differences across firms and studies examining differences within firms. Across firms, research should examine how aggregate levels of knowledge, motivation, and autonomy account for organizational-level differences in strategic activity and overall adaptive capability. Similarly, within firms, studies should investigate how differences in knowledge, motivation, and autonomy among midlevel actors account for differences in individuals' strategic behaviors. We now consider issues associated with cross-sectional research of this type.

Sampling

Both within and between levels of analysis require researchers to make decisions about which firms and managers to include in their studies. For firms, the theoretical boundaries discussed in the introduction suggest that samples should be large enough to require a legitimate cadre of midlevel professionals and that these firms should compete in relatively dynamic environments. In addition, for cross-firm studies, sample firms should be as similar as possible on dimensions likely to affect examined relationships. These include firm size, industry growth, technological complexity, and dynamism. Studies that use diverse samples, that include firms of different sizes, and/or that are drawn from several industries should be careful to incorporate appropriate controls so that they do not confound their results.

In addition, the individuals included in the study should be either the population of midlevel actors or a sample that represents all important functions and activities. Although these criteria seem straightforward, since the theoretical definition[1] of *midlevel professional* is somewhat ambiguous, the decision of who to include in a midlevel study requires significant judgment. As a first step, researchers should study the firm's organizational chart, making tentative decisions of who to include. Following this, one or more senior managers should be consulted for their reactions and suggestions.

Measurement

A number of studies have focused on and developed measures of the constructs in Table 7.1, including levels of trust within organizations (Tyler & Kramer, 1996), procedural and distributive justice (Folger &

Konovsky, 1989), organizational commitment (Porter, Steers, Mowday, & Boulian, 1974), managerial leadership style (Manz & Sims, 1990), and organizational culture (Trice & Beyer, 1993). In addition, the literature on TMT consensus (Bourgeois, 1980; Dess, 1987; Wooldridge & Floyd, 1989) provides guidance for assessing shared beliefs among individuals. For other constructs, most notably strategic knowledge, the field needs to develop theoretically anchored, reliable, and validated measures.

Even when measures exist, however, they should be seen as only a starting point. Researchers should carefully review—and, if necessary, modify—measures to ensure their consistency with the theoretical arguments being tested. In addition, in some cases, the development of context-specific measures may be desirable. In our own research (Wooldridge & Floyd, 1990), for example, we have found it useful to develop tailored measures to assess strategic understanding. To do this, we begin by interviewing several of a firm's managers about the company's strategy. From these responses, we develop measures that describe strategy in words familiar to respondents. Using this approach, we believe, not only avoids misinterpretations but also heightens the involvement of the study's participants.

In the research being discussed here, the constructs listed in Table 7.1 are envisioned as independent variables to be examined for their effects on strategic renewal. How best to assess the dependent variable (i.e., the process itself) depends on the specific nature of the study. For within-firm studies, the dependent variable may be a measure of individuals' strategic involvement or activity. In our own research, for example, we have used managers' self-reports of their involvement in the process (Wooldridge & Floyd, 1990) and how frequently they engage in various strategic behaviors (Floyd & Wooldridge, 1992, 1997). Future research might further develop this approach and consider the use of peer and top management assessments.

For cross-firm studies, the individual measures discussed above may be aggregated into organizational-level measures. Alternatively, more holistic measures rating the quality of the process may be appropriate. This type of rating may be arrived at through subjective assessments made by company officials or constituents. Top and middle-level managers, for example, may be polled for their assessment of how effective they believe a renewal activity to be. Knowledgeable outsiders, such as customers and analysts, may be polled as well for their appraisal of the company's renewal capability. In other cases, it may be more appropriate to use "objective" ratings (i.e., various performance measures). This, of course, needs to be justified on the basis that superior performance reflects a superior ability to adapt. It might be argued, for example, that among firms in industries that have undergone significant environmental shifts, long-term financial performance reflects adaptive capability.

Data Collection

The collection of data for process studies poses several significant challenges. First, in most cases, both organizational- and individual-level data are required. This necessitates the cooperation of numerous individuals within an organization. Since the nature of the questions asked might be viewed as threatening, it is probably not appropriate to merely distribute surveys. Rather, it is important that researchers proactively nurture respondents' interest and cooperation.

As a general rule, we believe the research process should begin with a series of interviews. First, one or more top managers should be queried for their general impressions and assessment of how strategy forms within the organization. Importantly, if top management's subjective assessment is to be used as an indicator of the effectiveness of the process, this information should be carefully documented in a way that can be meaningfully compared with other organizations. Second, interviews should be conducted with as many midlevel respondents as feasible. The purpose of these interviews is to allow the researcher to gain a feel for the organization's process and also to establish a rapport with respondents. During these interviews, respondents should be informed about the nature of the study and provided assurances of confidentiality. An overriding goal at this stage is to reduce potential response bias by setting the context for the study, hopefully raising participants' interest and lowering their suspicions.

Following the interviews, surveys may be administered in the formal data-gathering phase of the study. Although it may be convenient to have support staff distribute and collect surveys, in our opinion, this should be done by the researcher whenever possible. Collecting surveys allows researchers another chance to answer questions and address concerns. In addition, this approach minimizes any remaining confidentiality concerns.

As an alternative to surveys, researchers might consider the use of middle manager diaries. Balogun and Johnson (1998), for example, used diaries to study relationships between top management change efforts and middle management behavior. In the diaries, managers responded to five questions in the format of an unstructured questionnaire. By taking this more qualitative approach, they were able to develop insights into why and how deliberate implementation becomes unpredictable and emergent over time.

The potential for mono-method bias is another issue researchers should consider when designing their studies. Though we have found middle managers' self-reports to be relatively accurate and useful, it is not appropriate to obtain measures for both independent and dependent variables in this way. In a study investigating linkages between levels of organizational trust and managers' strategic involvement, for example, a manager reporting low levels of trust may be predisposed to also report low involvement. A more valid approach obtains each measure independently. In the present case, for example, a researcher might ask managers about their perceptions concerning levels of organizational trust and then gather data on involvement through other means such as top management reports, archival documents, or direct observation.

The Renewal-Performance Relationship

Theory

The linkage between midlevel strategy making and organizational performance is central to our motivation for writing this book. The top management perspective that has dominated the field has emphasized the deliberate side of strategy. As markets have become more dynamic and complex, however, the limitations of this approach have become increasingly apparent. Firms that rely on centralized decision making have had difficulty responding to continuous change. Commonly, strategic change follows a "punctuated equilibrium" (Gersick, 1991) pattern. These firms experience relatively long periods of strategic stability in which the effectiveness of the strategy, and hence performance, gradually declines over time. At some point, a crisis ensues, performance declines markedly, and radical, frame-breaking change is needed to rescue the firm from disaster (Tushman & Romanelli, 1985).

To a large degree, the interest in strategic renewal within the strategy field therefore reflects a need to avoid the performance declines and upheaval associated with crisis-driven change (Charkravarthy & Doz, 1992). In contrast to radical change, renewal is seen as a continuous, ongoing effort that keeps the firm aligned with its environment. Theoretically, as a complex adaptive system, the renewal process provides the firm with dynamic capability (Nelson, 1991; Teece, Pisano, & Shuen, 1997) that allows the firm to continually adapt to changing circumstances and, importantly, to maintain a more consistent level of performance. In theory, then, research should be able to demonstrate an association between characteristics of the renewal process and long-term organizational performance.

The problem is made more complex, however, by the fact that we have described the renewal process as a series of activities and interactions linked together by a common outcome (Van de Ven, 1992). This suggests that researchers must find ways to assess the activities or interactions as a collectivity, rather than as separate independent variables. This situation does not lend itself to multivariate statistical analysis employing a set of independent variables, yet qualitative methods are unlikely to be convincing as a basis for testing relationships to economic performance. Before suggesting alternatives to these research methodologies, however, we want to illustrate the kind of theoretical questions raised by the process-performance relationship.

High-Priority Research Issues

To conceptualize the relationship between a complex process like strategic renewal and organizational outcomes, we have decomposed it into more manageable pieces. In terms of the framework developed in Chapter 6, this means evaluating the relationships between the idea generation, initiative development, and integration stages of renewal and organizational performance. Simplifying the problem in this way helps to identify important research questions.

Without divergent ideas, the process of renewal never gets started. And we have argued that weak social ties, bridging relationships, deviant thinking, and motivation are important to the generation of ideas. An important question raised by this reasoning, however, is whether more is better, or, more precisely, just how much deviance can an organization tolerate before the situation degenerates into chaos or, more likely, into a complete political arena (Mintzberg, 1983)? Is there some way to assess the match between an organization's external environment and the level of internal cognitive diversity? Burgelman (1994) echoes many predecessors (Lawrence & Lorsch, 1967) when he suggests that the level of variety in the intraorganizational environment should match that in the external environment. Does this mean that variation, rather than degree, is the appropriate barometer for idea generation? Must ideas come from a variety of organizational actors, or can a variety of ideas come from a relatively narrow field of individual actors?

The second stage of renewal raises similar sorts of questions. We have argued that initiative development depends on the integration of conceptual and embodied knowledge, middle manager issue-selling behaviors, the presence of interpersonal trust, the behavior of middle-level central actors, and the development of emergent organizational routines. We have tried to show how these connect to one another over the life of an initiative, but there are still many unanswered theoretical questions about their role in creating competitive advantage. For example, what is the relationship between the number and diversity of issue sellers or central actors and organizational performance? Is the overall level of identification-based (strong-form) trust within the organization associated with organizational performance? Is the trustworthiness of central actors more important to organizational performance than the overall level of trust is?

The culmination of the renewal process is the integration and ratification of nascent capabilities. This process appears to rely on change in top management's belief system, shifting organizational politics, inclusion of top managers in emergent networks, norms within the top management team, clan controls, organizational memory, perceptions of equity, and rich information processing. In Chapter 6, we linked these factors but did not discuss how they might be related to organizational performance. For example, Dutton et al. (1997) suggest that top management's willingness to listen is important to issue selling. Does this mean that such a norm can be related to organizational performance? Similarly, how are perceptions of equity about renewal outcomes related to performance?

Questions like those raised in the last three paragraphs are troubling. In part, this is because they seem overly simplistic. Attempting to link variables such as the number of ideas generated within an organization or consensus within the top management team directly to competitive advantage seems a stretch at best. There are simply too many other related variables that interfere in such simple direct relationships. Unless we can link the renewal process to economic performance in some way, however, we will be unable to make normative statements or produce credible guidelines for practicing managers.

Appropriate Research Methods

Each stage of renewal can be represented as a complex combination of information flows, individual belief systems, social interactions, and organizational knowledge. One method that seems ideally suited to capture such phenomena in the aggregate in an organization over a period of time is social network analysis (Burt, 1982). Chapter 5 details the kind of measures and procedures used to represent social networks but does not really suggest how such an approach could be used in researching the relationships between a process like renewal and organizational performance.

It is possible to imagine a study, however, that tracks the idea-initiative-integration process for a number of strategic initiatives over a period of time within one organization or cross-sectionally for multiple organizations. On the basis of propositions like those in Chapter 6, it would be possible to compare the patterns that such an analysis would reveal with those that are theoretically related to successful renewal. One could observe, for example, whether new, divergent ideas come from a variety of organizational actors or from a particular social grouping. Then, given a sufficient number of observations, it would be possible to classify patterns in the evolution of social networks and relate these to organizational performance.

Similarly, it is possible to imagine a study that examines emergent patterns in the belief systems in organizations and compares these with organizational performance. For example, one could combine measures of the number, variety, and type of individual belief systems (i.e., cause maps) and compare these over time with organizational performance. Barr, Stimpert, and Huff (1992) used data from annual reports to compare the cause maps for the top management within two railroad companies, for example, and were able to show connections to organizational adaptiveness. Unfortunately, the cognitions of operating- and middle-level actors are not frequently represented in published documents. There may be other archival indicators of managers' thoughts, however, such as planning documents, presentations, memos, and electronic mail. Researchers may also need to rely on interview-based methodologies, such as repertory grid technique (Kelly, 1955), to elicit cause maps (Reger, 1990).

Naturally, the problem with moving the level of analysis from top management teams to the middle level of an organization is that the number of actors and relationships substantially increases. This creates an enormous data collection and analysis problem for cognitive analysis. Harnessing the power of the computer to collect questionnaire data or to content-analyze archival data (Huff & Fletcher, 1990) could solve such problems. Readers interested in pursuing this line of research should refer to Huff's (1990) volume for practical and detailed advice.

In summary, research on the relationship between particular characteristics of the strategic renewal process and organizational performance may be challenging, but it is not impossible.

Concluding Comment

As stated at the outset, the central assertion in this book is that much of what separates the performance of firms occurs not at the top but in the middle of organizations, and this is especially true in the present business climate. This proposition is consistent with the decentralization of strategic responsibilities adopted by an increasing number of top-level executives. In research and consulting, we have encountered firms in industries as diverse as insurance, pharmaceuticals, and chewing gum that expect strategic thinking and initiative from middle-level managers.

The primary purpose of this book, therefore, has been to synthesize and integrate theory and research that we believe connects to a middle-level perspective on strategy. In doing so, we have come to appreciate the richness of this literature and believe it reflects a growing recognition of the challenges posed by strategic renewal. Writing the book also made us aware that a middle-level perspective is only part of a broader reconceptualization of strategy process. Researchers pursuing this new line of work make different theoretical assumptions, ask different research questions, and employ a new vocabulary to frame the problem of strategy making. Thus, another thing we have tried to accomplish is to articulate the parameters of this emerging conversation.

We hope our synthesis stimulates and redirects the focus of strategy process research. Admittedly, the proposed agenda represents a formidable body of work. In our view, however, the potential payoffs are great. While research focusing at the top has created much valuable knowledge, it follows a well-worn path that may yield diminishing returns. In contrast, the relative scarcity of work focused at the middle suggests more fertile ground for future research.

Note

1. As defined in Chapter 1, we suggest that middle-level professionals are individuals entrusted by the firm with significant responsibilities who have access to top management and who possess significant operating know-how.

References

Abell, D. S., & Hammond, J. S. (1979). *Strategic market planning*. Englewood Cliffs, NJ: Prentice Hall.

Ackoff, R. L. (1970). *A concept of corporate planning*. New York: Wiley Interscience.

Adams, J. C. (1963). Toward an understanding of inequity. *Journal of Abnormal and Social Psychology, 67,* 422-436.

Aldrich, H. E. (1979). *Organizations and environments*. Englewood Cliffs, NJ: Prentice Hall.

Allison, G. (1971). *Essence of decision: Explaining the Cuban missile crisis*. New York: Little, Brown.

Amit, R., & Schoemaker, P. (1993). Strategic assets and organizational rent. *Strategic Management Journal, 14,* 33-46.

Andrews, K. (1971). *The concept of corporate strategy*. Homewood, IL: Irwin.

Ansoff, H. I. (1965). *Corporate strategy*. New York: McGraw-Hill.

Argyris, C., & Schon, D. (1978). *Organizational learning: A theory of action perspective*. Reading, MA: Addison-Wesley.

Ashkenas, R., Ulrich, D., Jick, T., & Kerr, S. (1992). *The boundaryless organization: Breaking the chains of organizational structure*. San Francisco: Jossey-Bass.

Bacharach, S. B. (1989). Organizational theories: Some criteria for evaluation. *Academy of Management Review, 14,* 496-515.

Balogun, J., & Johnson, G. (1998). Bridging the gap between intended and unintended change: The role of managerial sensemaking. In M. A. Hitt, J. E. Ricart, I. Costa, & R. D. Nixon (Eds.), *New managerial mindsets: Organizational transformation and strategic implementation*. London: John Wiley.

Barber, B. (1983). *The logic and limits of trust.* New Brunswick, NJ: Rutgers University Press.

Barnard, C. I. (1938). *The functions of the executive.* Cambridge, MA: Harvard University Press.

Barnett, W. P., & Burgelman, R. A. (1996). Evolutionary perspectives on strategy. *Strategic Management Journal, 17* [Special issue], 5-19.

Barney, J. (1986). Strategic factor markets: Expectations, luck, and business strategy. *Management Science, 42,* 1231-1241.

Barney, J. (1991). Firm resources and sustained competitive advantage. *Journal of Management, 17,* 99-120.

Barney, J. (1992). Integrating organizational behavior and strategy formulation research: A resource based analysis. In P. Shrivastava, A. Huff, & J. Dutton (Eds.), *Advances in strategic management, 8* (pp. 39-62). Greenwich, CT: JAI.

Barney, J. (1996). *Gaining and sustaining competitive advantage.* Reading, MA: Addison-Wesley.

Barney, J., & Hansen, M. H. (1994). Trustworthiness as a source of competitive advantage. *Strategic Management Journal, 15,* 175-190.

Barr, P. S., Stimpert, J. L., & Huff, A. S. (1992). Cognitive change, strategic action, and organizational renewal. *Strategic Management Journal, 13,* 15-36.

Bartlett, C. A., & Ghoshal, S. (1993). Beyond the M-form: Toward a managerial theory of the firm. *Strategic Management Journal, 14* [Special issue], 23-46.

Boje, D. M., & Whetten, D. A. (1981). Effects of organizational strategies and contextual constraints on centrality and attributions of influence in interorganizational networks. *Administrative Science Quarterly, 26,* 378-395.

Bourgeois, L. J., III. (1980). Performance and consensus. *Strategic Management Journal, 1,* 227-248.

Bourgeois, L. J., III. (1985). Strategic goals, perceived uncertainty, and economic performance in volatile environments. *Academy of Management Journal, 28,* 548-573.

Bourgeois, L. J., & Singh, J. (1983). Organizational slack and political behavior within top management teams. *Academy of Management Proceedings,* 43-47.

Bower, J. L. (1970). *Managing the resource allocation process.* Boston: Harvard Business School.

Bower, J. L. (1974). Planning and control: Bottom-up or top-down. *Journal of General Management, 1,* 20-31.

Bower, J. L., & Doz, I. (1979). Strategy formulation: A social and political view. In D. Schendel & C. Hofer (Eds.), *Strategic management.* Boston: Little, Brown.

Bowman, C., & Ambrosini, V. (1997). Perceptions of strategic priorities, consensus, and firm performance. *Journal of Management Studies, 34,* 241-258.

Brass, D. J. (1984). Being in the right place: A structural analysis of individual difference in an organization. *Administrative Science Quarterly, 29,* 518-539.

Brass, D. J., & Burkhardt, M. E. (1992). Centrality and power in organizations. In N. Nohria & R. G. Eccles (Eds.), *Networks and organizations* (pp. 191-215). Boston: Harvard Business School Press.

Braybrooke, D., & Lindblom, C. E. (1963). *A strategy of decision: Policy evaluation as a social process.* New York: New York University Press.

Brodwin, D. R., & Bourgeois, L. J., III. (1984). Five steps to strategic action. *California Management Review, 26,* 176-190.

Bromiley, P., & Cummings, L. L. (1992). *Transactions cost in organizations with trust* (Discussion Paper No. 128). Minneapolis: University of Minnesota, Minneapolis, Strategic Management Research Center.

Brown, S. L., & Eisenhardt, K. M. (1997). The art of continuous change: Linking time-based evolution in relentlessly shifting environments. *Administrative Science Quarterly, 42,* 1-34.

Buchholtz, A. K., & Ribbens, B. A. (1994). Role of chief executive officers in takeover resistance: Effects of CEO incentives and individual characteristics. *Academy of Management Journal, 3,* 554-579.

Burgelman, R. A. (1983a). A model of the interaction of strategic behavior, corporate context, and the concept of strategy. *Academy of Management Review, 8,* 61-70.

Burgelman, R. A. (1983b). A process model of the internal corporate venturing in the diversified major firm. *Administrative Science Quarterly, 28,* 223-244.

Burgelman, R. A. (1983c). Corporate entrepreneurship and strategic management: Insights from a process study. *Management Science, 29,* 1349-1364.

Burgelman, R. A. (1988). Strategy making as a social learning process: The case of internal corporate venturing. *Interfaces, 18,* 74-85.

Burgelman, R. A. (1991). Intraorganizational ecology of strategy making and organizational adaptation: Theory and field research. *Organization Science, 2,* 239-262.

Burgelman, R. A. (1994). Fading memories: A process theory of strategic business exits in dynamic environments. *Administrative Science Quarterly, 39,* 24-56.

Burgelman, R. A. (1996). A process model of strategic business exit: Implications for an evolutionary perspective. *Strategic Management Journal, 17* [Special issue], 193-214.

Burrell, G., & Morgan, G. (1979). *Sociological paradigms and organisational analysis: Elements of the society of corporate life.* London: Heinemann.

Burt, R. S. (1982). *Toward a structural theory of action: Network models of social structure, perception, and action.* New York: Academic Press.

Burt, R. S. (1983). *Corporate profits and cooptation.* New York: Academic Press.

Burt, R. S. (1992a). The social structure of competition. In N. Nohria & R. G. Eccles (Eds.), *Networks in organizations* (pp. 57-91). Boston: Harvard Business School Press.

Burt, R. S. (1992b). *Structural holes: The social structure of competition.* Cambridge, MA: Harvard University Press.

Butler, J. K., Jr., & Cantrell, R. S. (1984). A behavioral decision theory approach to modeling dyadic trust in superiors and subordinates. *Psychological Reports, 55,* 19-28.

Buzzell, R. D., Gale, B. T., & Sultan, R. (1975). Market share: A key to profitability. *Harvard Business Review, 51,* 97-106.

Calori, R., Johnson, G., & Sarnin, P. (1994). CEO's cognitive maps and the scope of the organization. *Strategic Management Journal, 15,* 437-457.

Carter, E. E. (1971). The behavioral theory of the firm and top-level corporate decisions. *Administrative Sciences Quarterly, 16,* 413-428.

Chakravarthy, B. S., & Doz, Y. (1992). Strategy process research: Focusing on corporate self-renewal. *Strategic Management Journal, 13* [Special issue], 5-14.

Chandler, A. D. (1962). *Strategy and structure: Chapters in the history of the American industrial enterprise.* Cambridge: MIT Press.

Chandler, A. D. (1989). *Strategy and structure: Chapters in the history of the American industrial enterprise.* Cambridge: MIT Press. (Original work published 1962)

Chandler, A. D. (1991). The functions of HQ unit in the multibusiness firm. *Strategic Management Journal, 12,* 31-50.

Chappell, D. S., & Huff, A. S. (1998). *Analysis and politics: A dual framework for understanding strategic decision processes* (Working paper).

Child, J. (1972). Organizational structure, environment, and performance: The role of strategic choice. *Sociology, 6,* 1-22.

Christensen, C. R., Andrews, K. R., Bower, J. L., Hamermesh, R. G., & Porter, M. E. (1982). *Business policy: Text and cases.* Homewood, IL: Irwin.

Clark, K. B., & Fujimoto, T. (1991). *Product development performance: Strategy, organization, and management in the world auto industry.* Boston: Harvard University Press.

Coase, R. H. (1937). The nature of the firm. *Economica, 4,* 386-405.

Cohen, M. D., March, J. G., & Olsen, J. P. (1972). A garbage can model of organizational choice. *Administrative Science Quarterly, 17,* 1-25.

Cohen, W., & Levinthal, D. (1990). Absorptive capacity: A new perspective on learning and innovation. *Administrative Science Quarterly, 35,* 128-152.

Collis, D. J. (1994). How valuable are organizational capabilities? *Strategic Management Journal, 15* [Special issue], 143-152.

Collis, D. J., & Montgomery, C. C. (1997). *Corporate strategy: Resources and the scope of the firm.* Chicago: McGraw-Hill.

Conner, K. (1991). A historical comparison of resource-based theory and five schools of thought within industrial organization economics: Do we have a new theory of the firm? *Journal of Management, 17,* 121-154.

Conner, K., & Prahalad, C. K. (1996). A resource-based theory of the firm: Knowledge versus opportunism. *Organizational Science, 7,* 477-501.

Cook, K. S., Emerson, R. M., Gillmore, M. R., & Yamagishi, T. (1983). The distribution of power in exchange networks: Theory and experimental results. *American Journal of Sociology, 89,* 275-305.

Cool, K., & Schendel, D. (1987). Strategic group formation and performance: The case of the U.S. pharmaceutical industry, 1963-1982. *Management Science, 33*(9), 1-23.

Creed, D., & Miles, R. (1996). A conceptual framework linking organizational forms, managerial philosophies, and the opportunity costs of controls. In R. Kramer & T. Tyler (Eds.), *Trust in organizations* (pp. 16-38). Thousand Oaks, CA: Sage.

Cyert, R. M., & March, J. G. (1963). *A behavioral theory of the firm.* Englewood Cliffs, NJ: Prentice Hall.

Daft, R. L., & Lengel, R. H. (1986). Organizational information requirements, media richness, and structural design. *Management Science, 5,* 554-571.

Daft, R. L., & Weick, K. E. (1984). Toward a model of organizations as interpretation systems. *Academy of Management Review, 9,* 284-295.

D'Aveni, R. A. (1994). *Hypercompetition.* New York: Free Press.

Davis, J. C. (1969). Toward a theory of revolutionary change. *American Sociological Review, 27,* 5-19.

Dean, J. N., & Sharfman, M. P. (1992). Procedural rationality in the strategic decision making process. *Journal of Management Studies, 30,* 607-630.

Dearborn, D. C., & Simon, H. A. (1958). Selective perception: A note on the departmental identification of the executive. *Sociometry, 21,* 140-144.

Denzin, N. K., & Lincoln, Y. S. (1994). *Handbook of qualitative research.* Thousand Oaks, CA: Sage.

Dess, G. (1987). Consensus on strategy formulation and organizational performance: Competitors in a fragmented industry. *Strategic Management Journal, 8,* 259-277.

Dess, G., & Origer, N. (1987). Environment, structure, and consensus in strategy formulation: A conceptual integration. *Academy of Management Review, 12,* 313-330.

Dess, G., & Priem, R. L. (1995). Consensus-performance research: Theoretical and empirical extensions. *Journal of Management Studies, 32,* 401-417.

Deutsch, K. W. (1958). *Science and the creative spirit: Essays on humanistic aspects of science.* Toronto: University of Toronto Press.

Dierickx, I., & Cool, K. (1989). Asset stock accumulation and sustainability of competitive advantage. *Management Science, 35,* 1504-1511.

DiMaggio, P. (1988). Interest and agency in institutional theory. In L. G. Zucker (Ed.), *Institutional patterns and organizations: Culture and environment* (pp. 3-21). Cambridge, MA: Ballinger.

DiMaggio, P., & Powell, W. W. (1983). The iron cage revisited: Institutional isomorphism and collective rationality in organizational fields. *American Sociological Review, 48,* 147-160.

Doz, Y. L. (1996). The evolution of cooperation in strategic alliances: Initial conditions or learning processes. *Strategic Management Journal, 17* [Special issue], 55-84.

Dubin, R. (1976). Theory building in applied areas. In M. D. Dunnette (Ed.), *Handbook of industrial and organizational psychology* (pp. 17-39). Chicago: Rand McNally.

Durkheim, E. (1933). *The division of labor in society.* New York: Macmillan.

Dutton, J. E., & Ashford, S. J. (1993). Selling issues to top management. *Academy of Management Review, 18,* 397-428.

Dutton, J. E., Ashford, S. J., O'Neill, R. M., Hayes, E., & Wierba, E. E. (1997). Reading the wind: How middle managers assess the context for selling issues to top managers. *Strategic Management Journal, 18,* 407-425.

Dutton, J. E., & Dukerich, J. M. (1991). Keeping one eye on the mirror: The role of image and identity in organizational adaptation. *Academy of Management Journal, 34,* 517-554.

Dutton, J. E., & Duncan, R. B. (1987). The creation of momentum for change through the process of strategic issue diagnosis. *Strategic Management Journal, 8*(3), 279-295.

Dutton, J. E., Fahey, L., & Narayanan, V. K. (1983). Toward understanding strategic issue diagnosis. *Strategic Management Journal, 4,* 307-323.

Dutton, J. E., & Jackson, S. B. (1987). Categorizing strategic issues: Links to organizational action. *Academy of Management Review, 12,* 76-90.

Dutton, J. E., & Ottensmeyer, E. (1987). Strategic issue management systems: Forms, functions, and contexts. *Academy of Management Review, 12,* 355-365.

Egelhoff, W. (1988). *Organizing the multinational enterprise: An information processing perspective.* Cambridge, MA: Ballinger.

Eisenhardt, K. M. (1989). Building theories from case study research. *Academy of Management Review, 14,* 532-550.

Eisenhardt, K. M., & Bourgeois, L. J., III. (1988). Politics of strategic decision making in high velocity environments: Towards a midrange theory. *Academy of Management Journal, 31,* 737-770.

Eisenhardt, K. M., & Zbaracki, M. J. (1992, Winter). Strategic decision making. *Strategic Management Journal, 13* [Special issue], 17-37.

Feldman, M. S. (1989). *Order without design.* Stanford, CA: Stanford University Press.

Fiol, C. M. (1989). A semiotic analysis of corporate language: Organizational boundaries and joint venturing. *Administrative Science Quarterly, 34,* 277-303.

Floyd, S. W., & Wooldridge, B. (1992). Middle management involvement in strategy and its association with strategic type. *Strategic Management Journal, 13,* 153-167.

Floyd, S. W., & Wooldridge, B. (1996). *The strategic middle manager: How to create and sustain competitive advantage.* San Francisco: Jossey-Bass.

Floyd, S. W., & Wooldridge, B. (1997). Middle managers' strategic influence and organizational performance. *Journal of Management Studies, 34,* 465-485.

Floyd, S. W., & Wooldridge, B. (1999, Spring). Knowledge creation and social networks in corporate entrepreneurship: The renewal of organizational capability. *Entrepreneurship: Theory and Practice, 23,* 1-21.

Folger, R., & Konovsky, M. K. (1989). Effects of procedural and distributive justice on reactions to pay raise decisions. *Academy of Management Journal, 32,* 115-130.

Fredrickson, J. (1984). The competitiveness of strategic decision processes: Extension, observations, future directions. *Academy of Management Journal, 27,* 445-466.

Fredrickson, J., & Mitchell, T. (1984). Strategic decision processes: Comprehensiveness and performance in an industry with an unstable environment. *Academy of Management Journal, 27,* 399-423.

Freeman, L. (1979). Centrality in social networks: Conceptual clarification. *Social Networks, 1,* 215-239.

Friedkin, N. (1980). A test of structural features of Granovetter's "strength of weak ties" theory. *Social Networks, 2,* 22-41.

Frost, P. (1995). *Publishing in the organizational sciences.* Thousand Oaks, CA: Sage.

Gabarro, J. J. (1978). The development of trust, influence, and expectation. In A. G. Athos & J. J. Gabarro (Eds.), *Interpersonal behavior: Communication and understanding in relationships* (pp. 290-303). Englewood Cliffs, NJ: Prentice Hall.

Galaskiewicz, J., & Wasserman, S. (1993). Social network analysis: Concepts, methodology, and directions for the nineties. *Sociological Methods and Research, 22,* 3-22.

Galbraith, J. (1977). *Organizational design.* Reading, MA: Addison-Wesley.

Galbraith, J., & Kazanjian, R. (1986). *Strategy implementation* (2nd ed.). St. Paul, MN: West.

Gersick, C. J. G. (1991). Revolutionary change theories: A multi-level exploration of the punctuated equilibrium paradigm. *Academy of Management Review, 32,* 274-309.

Gilbert, X., & Lorange, P. (1974, Fall). Five pillars for your planning. *European Business, 33,* 82-90.

Gioia, D. A., & Chittipeddi, K. (1991). Sensemaking and sensegiving in strategic change initiation. *Strategic Management Journal, 12,* 433-448.

Glade, W. P. (1967, Spring/Summer). Approaches to a theory of entrepreneurial formation. *Explorations in Entrepreneurial History, 4*(3), 245-259.

Granovetter, M. S. (1973). The strength of weak ties. *American Journal of Sociology, 78,* 1360-1380.

Granovetter, M. S. (1974). *Getting a job: A study of contacts and careers.* Cambridge, MA: Harvard University Press.

Grant, R. M. (1991). The resource-based theory of competitive advantage: Implications for strategy formulation. *California Management Review, 33,* 114-135.

Grant, R. M. (1996, Winter). Toward a knowledge-based theory of the firm. *Strategic Management Journal, 17* [Special issue], 109-122.

Greenberg, J. (1986). Determinants of perceived fairness of performance evaluations. *Journal of Applied Psychology, 71,* 340-342.

Grinyer, P., & Norburn, D. (1977-1978). Planning for existing markets: An empirical study. *International Studies in Management and Organization, 7,* 99-122.

Grinyer, P. H., & Spender, J. C. (1979). Recipes, crises, and adaptation in mature businesses. *International Studies of Management and Organization, 9,* 113-123.

Guth, W. D., & MacMillan, I. C. (1986). Strategy implementation versus middle manager self-interest. *Strategic Management Journal, 7,* 313-327.

Hambrick, D. C. (1984). Taxonomic approaches to studying strategy: Some conceptual and methodological issues. *Journal of Management, 10,* 27-41.

Hambrick, D. C. (1987). Top management teams: Key to strategic success. *California Management Review, 30,* 88-108.

Hambrick, D. C. (1988). Guest editor's introduction: Putting top managers back in the strategy picture. *Strategic Management Journal, 10,* 5-15.

Hambrick, D. C., & Mason, P. A. (1984). Upper echelons: The organization as a reflection of its top managers. *Academy of Management Review, 9,* 193-206.

Hamel, G., & Prahalad, C. K. (1989, May/June). Strategic intent. *Harvard Business Review,* 63-76.

Hannan, M. T., & Freeman, J. (1977). The population ecology of organizations. *American Journal of Sociology, 82,* 929-964.

Hart, S. (1992). An integrative framework for strategy-making processes. *Academy of Management Review, 17,* 327-351.

Hart, S. L., & Banbury, C. (1994). How strategy making process can make a difference. *Strategic Management Journal, 15,* 251-269.

Hayes, R. H., & Pisano, G. P. (1994). Beyond world-class: The new manufacturing strategy. *Harvard Business Review, 72*(1), 77-87.

Hinings, C. R., Hickson, D. J., Pennings, J. M., & Schneck, R. E. (1974). Structural conditions of intraorganizational power. *Administrative Science Quarterly, 19,* 21-44.

Hofer, C. (1975). Toward a contingency theory of business strategy. *Academy of Management Journal, 18,* 784-810.

Holland, J. K. (1975). *Adaptation in natural and artificial systems.* Ann Arbor: University of Michigan Press.

Holub, M. (1977, February 4). Brief thoughts on maps. *Times Literary Supplement,* p. 118.

Hosmer, L. T. (1995). Trust: The connecting link between organizational theory and philosophical ethics. *Academy of Management Review, 20,* 379-403.

Hrebiniak, L. G., & Joyce, W. F. (1984). *Implementing strategy.* New York: Macmillan.

Hrebiniak, L. G., & Snow, C. C. (1982). Top management agreement and organizational performance. *Human Relations, 35,* 1139-1158.

Huber, G. (1991). Organizational learning: The contributing processes and the literatures. *Organizational Science, 2,* 88-115.

Huff, A. S. (1990). Mapping strategic thought. In A. S. Huff (Ed.), *Mapping strategic thought* (pp. 11-49). New York: John Wiley.

Huff, A. S., & Fletcher, K. E. (1990). Conclusion: Key mapping decisions. In A. S. Huff (Ed.), *Mapping strategic thought* (pp. 403-412). New York: John Wiley.

Huff, J. O., & Huff, A. S. (2000). *A cognitively anchored theory of strategic change.* Oxford, UK: Oxford University Press.

Huff, J. O., Huff, A. S., & Thomas, H. (1992). Strategic renewal and the interaction of cumulative stress and inertia. *Strategic Management Journal, 13,* 55-75.

Hurst, D. K., Rush, J. C., & White, R. E. (1989). Top management team and organizational renewal. *Strategic Management Journal, 10,* 87-105.

Hutt, M. D., Reingen, P. H., & Ronchetto, J. R., Jr. (1988). Tracing emergent processes in marketing strategy formation. *Journal of Marketing, 52,* 4-19.

Ibarra, H. (1993). Network centrality, power, and innovation involvement: Determinants of technical and administrative roles. *Academy of Management Journal, 36,* 471-501.

Jain, S. (1989). Standardization of international marketing strategy. *Journal of Marketing, 53,* 70-79.

Janis, I. L. (1972). *Victims of groupthink.* Boston: Houghton Mifflin.

Johnson, G. (1987). *Strategic change and the management process.* Oxford, UK: Basil Blackwell.

Johnson, G. J. (1988). Rethinking incrementalism. *Strategic Management Journal, 9,* 75-91.

Johnson, G. J., & Huff, A. S. (1998). Everyday innovation, everyday strategy. In G. Hamel, C. K. Prahalad, H. Thomas, & D. O'Neal (Eds.), *Strategic flexibility: Managing in a turbulent environment* (pp. 13-28). Chichester, UK: Wiley.

Kanter, R. M. (1982). The middle manager as innovator. *Harvard Business Review, 60,* 95-105.

Kanter, R. M. (1983). *The change masters.* New York: Basic Books.

Kauffman, S. A. (1995). *At home in the universe: The search for laws of self-organization and complexity.* New York: Oxford University Press.

Kelly, G. A. (1955). *The psychology of personal constructs* (Vols. 1-2). New York: Norton.

Keys, B., & Bell, R. (1982). Four faces of the fully functioning middle manager. *California Management Review, 14,* 59-67.

Kidder, T. (1981). *The soul of a new machine.* Boston: Little, Brown.

Kiesler, S., & Sproull, L. (1982). Managerial response to changing environments: Perspectives on problem sensing from social cognition. *Administration Science Quarterly, 27,* 548-570.

Kogut, B., & Zander, U. (1992). Knowledge of the firm, combinative capabilities, and the replication of technology. *Organizational Science, 3,* 383-397.

Kogut, B., & Zander, U. (1993). Knowledge of the firm and the evolutionary theory of the multinational corporation. *Journal of International Business Studies, 24,* 625-646.

Kogut, B., & Zander, U. (1995). Knowledge, market failure, and the multinational enterprise: A reply. *Journal of International Business Studies, 26,* 417-426.

Krackhardt, D. (1992). The strength of strong ties: The importance of *philos* in organizations. In N. Nohria & R. G. Eccles (Eds.), *Networks and organizations* (pp. 216-239). Boston: Harvard Business School Press.

Krackhardt, D., & Stern, R. (1988). Informal networks and organizational crisis: An experimental simulation. *Social Psychology Quarterly, 51,* 123-140.

Kramer, R. M. (1993). Cooperation and organizational identification. In J. K. Murnighan (Ed.), *Social psychology in organizations: Advances in theory and research* (pp. 244-268). Englewood Cliffs, NJ: Prentice Hall.

Kuhn, T. S. (1962). *The structure of scientific revolutions.* Chicago: University of Chicago Press.

LaBianca, G., Brass, D. J., & Gray, B. (1998). Social networks and perceptions of intergroup conflict: The role of negative relationships and third parties. *Academy of Management Journal, 41,* 55-67.

Lane, P. J., & Lubatkin, M. (1998). Relative absorptive capacity and interorganizational learning. *Strategic Management Journal, 19,* 461-476.

Lawrence, P., & Lorsch, J. (1967). *Organization and environment.* Boston: Harvard Business School Press.

Learned, E. P., Christensen, R. C., Andrews, K., & Guth, W. (1965). *Business policy: Text and cases.* Homewood, IL: Irwin.

Lee, T. (1998). *Using qualitative methods in organizational research.* Thousand Oaks, CA: Sage.

Leonard-Barton, D. (1992). Core capabilities and core rigidities: A paradox in managing new product development. *Strategic Management Journal, 13,* 111-125.

Levinthal, D. A., & March, J. G. (1993). The myopia of learning. *Strategic Management Journal, 14,* 95-112.

Levitt, B., & Nass, C. (1989). The lid on the garbage can: Institutional constraints on decision making in the technical care of college-text publishers. *Administrative Sciences Quarterly, 34,* 190-207.

Lewicki, R. J., & Bunker, B. B. (1996). Developing and maintaining trust in work relationships. In R. M. Kramer & T. R. Tyler (Eds.), *Trust in organizations: Frontiers of theory and research* (pp. 114-139). Thousand Oaks, CA: Sage.

Lin, N., Dayton, P. W., & Greenwald, P. (1978). Analyzing the instrumental use of relations in the context of social structure. *Sociological Methods and Research, 7,* 149-166.

Lincoln, J. R. (1982). Intra- (and inter-) organizational networks. *Research in the Sociology of Organizations, 1,* 1-38.

Lind, E. A., & Tyler, T. R. (1988). *The social psychology of procedural justice.* New York: Plenum.

Lindblom, C. E. (1959). The science of "muddling through." *Public Administrative Review, 19,* 79-88.

Lippman, S. A., & Rumelt, R. P. (1982). Uncertain imitability: An analysis of interfirm differences in efficiency under competition. *Bell Journal of Economics, 13,* 418-438.

Lorange, P., & Vancil, R. F. (Eds.). (1977). *Strategic planning systems.* Englewood Cliffs, NJ: Prentice Hall.

Lorenz, E. H. (1988). Neither friends nor strangers: Informal networks of subcontracting in French industry. In D. Gambetta (Ed.), *Trust: Making and breaking cooperative relations* (pp. 194-210). Oxford, UK: Basil Blackwell.

Louis, M. (1980). Surprise and sense making: What newcomers experience in entering unfamiliar organizational settings. *Administrative Sciences Quarterly, 25,* 226-251.

Luhmann, N. (1988). Familiarity, confidence, trust: Problems and alternatives. In D. Gambetta (Ed.), *Trust: Making and breaking cooperative relations* (pp. 94-108). Oxford, UK: Basil Blackwell.

Lyles, M. A., & Mitroff, I. I. (1980). Organizational problem formulation: An empirical study. *Administrative Sciences Quarterly, 25,* 109-119.

MacMillan, I. C. (1978). *Strategy formulation: Political concepts.* St. Paul, MN: West.

Magjuka, R. (1988). Garbage can theory of decision making: A review. *Research in Sociology of Organizations, 6,* 225-259.

Manz, C. C., & Sims, H., Jr. (1990). *Superleadership: Leading others to lead themselves.* New York: Berkley.

March, J. G. (1962). The business firm as a political coalition. *Journal of Politics, 24,* 662-678.

March, J. G. (1981). Footnotes to organizational change. *Administrative Sciences Quarterly, 26,* 563-577.

March, J. G., & Simon, H. A. (1958). *Organizations.* New York: John Wiley.

Markoczy, L. (1997). Measuring beliefs: Accept no substitutes. *Academy of Management Journal, 40,* 1228-1242.

Markovsky, B., Willer, D., & Patton, T. (1988). Power relations in exchange networks. *American Sociological Review, 53,* 220-236.

Marshall, C., & Rossman, G. B. (1989). *Designing qualitative research.* Newbury Park, CA: Sage.

Mascarenhas, B., & Aaker, D. A. (1989). Mobility barriers and strategic groups. *Strategic Management Journal, 10,* 475-485.

Mead, G. H. (1956). *The social psychology of George Herbert Mead* (A. M. Strauss, Ed.). Chicago: University of Chicago Press.

Mehra, A. (1996). Resource and market based determinants of performance in the U.S. banking industry. *Strategic Management Journal, 17,* 307-322.

Michel, J. G., & Hambrick, D. C. (1992). Diversification posture and top management team characteristics. *Academy of Management Journal, 35,* 9-38.

Micklewait, J., & Wooldridge, A. (1996). *The witch doctors: Making sense of the management gurus.* New York: Random House.

Miles, M. B., & Huberman, A. M. (1994). *Qualitative data analysis.* Thousand Oaks, CA: Sage.

Miles, R. E., & Snow, C. C. (1978). *Organizational strategy, structure, and process.* New York: McGraw-Hill.

Miller, C. C., & Cardinal, L. B. (1994). Strategic planning and firm performance: A synthesis of more than two decades of research. *Academy of Management Journal, 37,* 1649-1665.

Miller, D., Kets de Vries, M. F., & Toulouse, J. M. (1982). Top executive locus of control and its relationship to strategy-making, structure, and environment. *Academy of Management Journal, 25,* 237-253.

Miller, D., & Shamsie, J. (1996). The resource-based view of the firm in tow environments: The Hollywood film, studios from 1936-1965. *Academy of Management Journal, 39,* 519-543.

Mintzberg, H. (1972). *Research on strategy-making.* Paper presented at the 32nd annual meeting of the Academy of Management, Minneapolis, MN.

Mintzberg, H. (1978). Patterns in strategy formation. *Management Science, 24,* 934-948.

Mintzberg, H. (1983). *Power in and around organizations.* Englewood Cliffs, NJ: Prentice Hall.

Mintzberg, H. (1990). The design school: Reconsidering the basic premises of strategic management. *Strategic Management Journal, 11,* 171-195.

Mintzberg, H., & McHugh, A. (1985). Strategy formation in an adhocracy. *Administrative Science Quarterly, 30*(2), 160-197.

Mintzberg, H., Raisinghani, D., & Theoret, A. (1976). The structure of "unstructured" decision processes. *Administrative Sciences Quarterly, 21,* 246-275.

Mintzberg, H., & Waters, J. (1982). Tracking strategy in an entrepreneurial firm. *Academy of Management Journal, 25,* 465-499.

Mintzberg, H., & Waters, J. (1984). Researching the formation of strategies: The history of Canadian lady, 1939-1976. In R. Lamb (Ed.), *Competitive strategic management.* Englewood Cliffs, NJ: Prentice Hall.

Mintzberg, H., & Waters, J. (1985). Of strategies deliberate and emergent. *Strategic Management Journal, 6,* 257-272.

Mishra, A. K. (1996). Organizational responses to crisis: The centrality of trust. In R. M. Kramer & T. R. Tyler (Eds.), *Trust in organizations: Frontiers of theory and research* (pp. 261-287). Thousand Oaks, CA: Sage.

Mizruchi, M. S. (1992). *The structure of corporate political action: Interfirm relations and their consequences.* Cambridge, MA: Harvard University Press.

Mizruchi, M. S. (1993). Cohesion, equivalence, and similarity of behavior: A theoretical and empirical assessment. *Social Networks, 15,* 275-307.

Mizruchi, M. S. (1994). Social network analysis: Recent achievements and current controversies. *Acta Sociologica, 37,* 329-343.

Narayanan, V. K., & Fahey, L. (1982). The micropolitics of strategy formulation. *Academy of Management Review, 7,* 25-34.

Nelson, R. (1991). Why do firms differ, and how does it matter? *Strategic Management Journal, 12,* 61-74.

Nelson, R., & Winter, S. (1982). *An evolutionary theory of economic change.* Cambridge, MA: Harvard University Press.

Nisbett, R. E., & Ross, L. (1980). *Human inference.* Englewood Cliffs, NJ: Prentice Hall.

Nohria, N., & Eccles, R. G. (Eds.). (1992). *Networks and organizations: Structure, form, and action.* Boston: Harvard Business School Press.

Nonaka, I. (1988). Toward middle-up-down management: Accelerating information creation. *Sloan Management Review, 29,* 9-18.

Nonaka, I. (1991). The knowledge-creating company. *Harvard Business Review, 69,* 96-104.

Nonaka, I. (1994). A dynamic theory of organizational knowledge creation. *Organization Science, 5,* 14-37.

Nonaka, I., & Takeuchi, H. (1995). *The knowledge-creating company: How Japanese companies create the dynamics of innovation.* New York: Oxford University Press.

Nutt, P. (1987). Identifying and appraising how managers install strategy. *Strategic Management Journal, 8,* 1-14.

Ouichi, W. G. (1980). Markets, bureaucracies, and clans. *Administrative Science Quarterly, 25,* 129-141.

Penrose, E. T. (1959). *The theory of the growth of the firm.* Oxford, UK: Basil Blackwell.

Peteraf, M. A. (1993). The cornerstones of competitive advantage: A resource based view. *Strategic Management Journal, 14,* 179-191.

Peters, T. (1987). *Thriving on chaos.* New York: Knopf.

Peters, T., & Waterman, R. (1980). *In search of excellence.* New York: HarperCollins.

Pettigrew, A. M. (1973). *The politics of organizational decision-making.* London: Tavistock.

Pettigrew, A. M. (1985). *The awakening giant: Continuity and change in ICI.* Oxford, UK: Basil Blackwell.

Pettigrew, A. M. (1992). On studying managerial elites. *Strategic Management Journal, 13,* 163-182.

Pfeffer, J. (1993). Barriers to the advance of organizational science: Paradigm development as a dependent variable. *Academy of Management Review, 18,* 599-620.

Pfeffer, J., & Salancik, G. R. (1978). *The external control of organizations: A resource dependence perspective.* New York: Harper & Row.

Polanyi, M. (1967). *The tacit dimension.* New York: Anchor Day Books.

Porter, L. M., Steers, R. M., Mowday, R. T., & Boulian, P. V. (1974). Organizational commitment, job satisfaction, and turnover among psychiatric technicians. *Journal of Applied Psychology, 59,* 603-609.

Porter, M. (1980). *Competitive strategy: Techniques for analyzing industries and competitors.* New York: Free Press.

Porter, M. (1985). *Competitive advantage.* New York: Free Press.

Porter, M. (1991). *The competitive advantage of nations.* New York: Free Press.

Prahalad, C. K., & Bettis, R. (1986). The dominant logic: A new linkage between diversity and performance. *Strategic Management Journal, 7,* 485-502.

Prahalad, C. K., & Hamel, G. (1990, May/June). The core competence of the corporation. *Harvard Business Review,* 79-91.

Priem, R. (1990). Top management team group factors, consensus, and performance. *Strategic Management Journal, 11,* 469-478.

Priem, R. L. (1992, Summer). An application of metric conjoint analysis for the evaluation of top managers' individual strategic decision making processes: A research note. *Strategic Management Journal, 13* [Special issue], 143-151.

Quinn, J. B. (1978, Fall). Strategic change: Logical incrementalism. *Sloan Management Review,* 7 -21.

Quinn, J. B. (1980). *Strategies for change: Logical incrementalism.* Homewood, IL: Irwin.

Reed, R., & DeFillippi, R. (1990). Causal ambiguity, barriers to imitation, and sustainable competitive advantage. *Academy of Management Review, 15,* 88-102.

Reger, R. K. (1990). The repertoiry grid technique for eliciting the content and structure of cognitive constructive systems. In A. S. Huff (Ed.), *Mapping strategic thought* (pp. 301-310). New York: John Wiley.

Reger, R. K., & Huff, A. S. (1993). Strategic groups: A cognitive approach. *Strategic Management Journal, 14,* 103-124.

Rousseau, D., Sitkin, S., Burt, R., & Camerer, C. (1998). Not so different after all: A cross discipline view of trust. *Academy of Management Review, 23,* 393-412.

Rumelt, R. P. (1974). *Strategy, structure, and economic performance.* Boston: Harvard University Press.

Rumelt, R. P., Schendel, D., & Teece, D. J. (1994, Winter). Strategic management and economics. *Strategic Management Journal, 12* [Special issue], 5-29.

Salancik, G. R., & Pfeffer, J. (1974). The bases and use of power in organizational decision making: The case of a university. *Administrative Science Quarterly, 19,* 453-473.

Sapienza, A. M. (1987). Imagery and strategy. *Journal of Management, 13,* 543-555.

Sayles, L. (1993). *The working leader.* New York: Free Press.

Schein, E. H. (1985). *Organizational culture and leadership.* San Francisco: Jossey-Bass.

Schendel, D. (1991, Summer). Introduction. *Strategic Management Journal, 12* [Special issue], 1-4.

Schendel, D., & Hofer, C. (1979). *Strategic management: A new view of business policy and planning.* Boston: Little, Brown.

Schoefler, S., Buzzell, R. D., & Heany, D. F. (1974). Impact of strategic planning on profit performance. *Harvard Business Review, 52,* 137-145.

Schweiger, D. M., & Sandberg, W. R. (1989). The utilization of individual capabilities in group approaches to strategic decision-making. *Strategic Management Journal, 10,* 31-43.

Schweiger, D. M., Sandberg, W. R., & Ragan, J. (1986). Group approaches for improving strategic decision making: A comparative analysis of dialectical inquiry, devil's advocacy, and consensus. *Academy of Management Journal, 29,* 51-71.

Schweiger, D. M., Sandberg, W. R., & Rechner, P. L. (1989). Experiential effects of dialectical inquiry, devil's advocacy, and consensus approaches to strategic decision making. *Academy of Management Journal, 32,* 745-772.

Schwenk, C. R. (1984). Effects of planning aids and presentation media on performance and affective responses in strategic decision making. *Management Science, 30,* 263-272.

Scott, W. R. (1995). *Institutions and organizations.* Thousand Oaks, CA: Sage.

Selznick, P. (1957). *Leadership in administration: A sociological interpretation.* New York: Harper & Row.

Senge, P. M. (1996, November). *Organizational learning.* Paper presented at the Annual International Conferences of the Strategic Management Society, Phoenix, AZ.

Shapiro, D., Sheppard, B. H., & Cheraskin, L. (1992). Business on a handshake. *Negotiation Journal, 8,* 365-377.

Simon, H. A. (1947). *Administrative behavior.* New York: Macmillan.

Simon, H. A. (1957). *The new science of management decision.* New York: Harper.

Singh, J. V. (1986). Performance, slack, and risk taking in organizational decision making. *Academy of Management Journal, 29,* 562-585.

Sloan, A. (1972). *My years with General Motors.* Garden City, NY: Doubleday.

Smircich, L., & Stubbart, C. (1985). Strategic management in an enacted world. *Academy of Management Review, 10,* 724-736.

Snow, C. C., & Hrebiniak, L. G. (1980). Strategy, distinctive competence, and organizational performance. *Administrative Sciences Quarterly, 25,* 317-336.

Spender, J. C. (1989). *Industry recipes: The nature and sources of managerial judgement.* Oxford, UK: Basil Blackwell.

Spender, J. C. (1996, Winter). Making knowledge the basis of a dynamic theory of the firm. *Strategic Management Journal, 17* [Special issue], 45-62.

Stacey, R. D. (1995). The science of complexity: An alternative perspective for strategic change processes. *Strategic Management Journal, 16,* 477-495.

Stagner, R. (1969). Corporate decision making: An empirical study. *Journal of Applied Psychology, 53,* 1-13.

Stalk, G., Evans, P., & Shulman, L. E. (1992). Competing on capabilities: The new rules of corporate strategy. *Harvard Business Review, 70*(2), 57-70.

Starbuck, W. H., & Milliken, F. J. (1988). Executives' perceptual filters: What they notice and how they make sense. In D. C. Hambrick (Ed.), *The executive effect: Concepts and methods for studying top managers* (pp. 35-65). Greenwich, CT: JAI.

Staw, B. M., McKechnie, P. I., & Puffer, S. M. (1993). The justification of organizational performance. *Administrative Science Quarterly, 28,* 582-600.

Steiner, G. A. (1970, September/October). Rise of the corporate planner. *Harvard Business Review, 48,* 133-139.

Subramaniam, M., & Venkatraman, N. (1998). *The influence of leveraging tacit overseas knowledge on global new product development capability: An empirical examination* (Working paper).

Sweeney, P. D., & McFarlin, D. B. (1993). Worker's evaluations of the "ends" and the "means": An examination of four models of distributive and procedural justice. *Organizational Behavior and Human Decision Processes, 55,* 23-37.

Szulanski, G. (1996, Winter). Exploring internal stickiness: Impediments to the transfer of best practice within the firm. *Strategic Management Journal, 17* [Special issue], 27-43.

Takeuchi, H., & Nonaka, I. (1986). The new product development game. *Harvard Business Review, 64,* 137-146.

Taylor, F. (1947). *Principles of scientific management.* New York: Harper.

Teece, D. J., Pisano, G., & Shuen, A. (1997). Dynamic capabilities and strategic management. *Strategic Management Journal, 18,* 509-533.

Tichy, N. M., Tushman, M. L., & Fombrun, C. (1979). Social network analysis for organizations. *Academy of Management Review, 4,* 507-519.

Tilles, S. (1963, July/August). How to evaluate corporate strategy. *Harvard Business Review,* 111-120.

Trice, H., & Beyer, J. (1993). *The cultures of work organizations.* Englewood Cliffs, NJ: Prentice Hall.

Tushman, M., Newman, W. H., & Romanelli, E. (1986, Fall). Convergence and upheaval: Managing the unsteady pace of organizational evolution. *California Management Review, 29*(1), 29-44.

Tushman, M., & Romanelli, E. (1985). Organizational evolution: A metamorphosis model of convergence and reorientation. In L. L. Cummings & B. M. Staw (Eds.), *Research in organizational behavior* (pp. 171-222). Greenwich, CT: JAI.

Tyler, R. M., & Kramer, T. R. (1996). *Trust in organizations: Frontiers of theory and research.* Thousand Oaks, CA: Sage.

Uyterhoven, H. E. R. (1972, March/April). General managers in the middle. *Harvard Business Review.*

Van de Ven, A. H. (1992, Summer). Suggestions for studying strategy process: A research note. *Strategic Management Journal, 13* [Special issue], 169-188.

Van de Ven, A. H., & Poole, S. M. (1995). Explaining development and change in organizations. *Academy of Management Review, 20,* 510-540.

Vancil, R. F. (1976, Winter). Strategy formulation in complex organizations. *Sloan Management Review, 17,* 1-18.

Vancil, R. F., & Lorange, P. (1975). Strategic planning in diversified companies. *Harvard Business Review, 53*(1), 149-158.

Venkataraman, S., MacMillan, I. C., & McGrath, R. C. (1992). Progress in research on corporate venturing. In D. L. Sexton & J. I. Kasarda (Eds.), *The state of the art of entrepreneurship* (pp. 487-519). Boston: PWS-Kent.

Waldrop, M. M. (1992). *Complexity: The emerging science at the edge of order and chaos.* New York: Simon & Schuster.

Walsh, J. P. (1995). Managerial and organizational cognition: Notes from a trip down memory lane. *Organization Science, 6,* 280-321.

Walsh, J. P., & Ungson, G. R. (1991). Organizational memory. *Academy of Management Review, 16,* 57-91.

Weber, M. (1947). *The theory of social and economic organization.* Glencoe, IL: Free Press.

Weick, K. E. (1979). *The social psychology of organizing.* Reading, MA: Addison-Wesley.

Weick, K. E. (1990). Introduction: Cartographic myths in organizations. In A. S. Huff (Ed.), *Mapping strategic thought* (pp. 1-10). New York: John Wiley.

Weick, K. E. (1995). *Sensemaking in organizations.* Thousand Oaks, CA: Sage.

Weick, K. E., & Bougon, M. (1986). Organizations as cognitive maps: Charting ways to success and failure. In H. P. Sims Jr. & D. A. Gioia & Associates (Eds.), *The thinking organization* (pp. 102-135). San Francisco: Jossey-Bass.

Wernerfelt, B. (1984). A resource based view of the firm. *Strategic Management Journal, 5,* 171-180.

Westley, F. (1990). Middle managers and strategy: Microdynamics of inclusion. *Strategic Management Journal, 11,* 337-351.

Whetten, D. A. (1988). Sources, responses, and effects of organizational decline. In K. S. Cameron, R. I. Sutton, & D. A. Whetten, *Readings in organizational decline* (pp. 151-174). Cambridge, MA: Ballinger.

White, M. C., Marin, D. B., Brazeal, D. V., & Friedman, W. H. (1997). The evolution of organizations: Suggestions from complexity theory about the interplay between natural selection and adaptation. *Human Relations, 50,* 1-19.

Wiersema, M., & Bantel, K. (1993). Top management team turnover as an adaptation mechanism: The role of the environment. *Strategic Management Journal, 14,* 485-504.

Wilkins, A. L., & Ouichi, W. G. (1983). Efficient cultures: Exploring the relationship between culture and organizational performance. *Administrative Science Quarterly, 28,* 468-481.

Williamson, O. E. (1975). *Markets and hierarchies: Analysis and antitrust implications.* New York: Free Press.

Wooldridge, B., & Floyd, S. W. (1989). Strategic process effects on consensus. *Strategic Management Journal, 10,* 295-302.

Wooldridge, B., & Floyd, S. W. (1990). The strategy process, middle management involvement, and organizational performance. *Strategic Management Journal, 11,* 231-241.

Yin, R. K. (1995). *Case study research: Design and methods.* Thousand Oaks, CA: Sage.

Zander, U., & Kogut, B. (1995). Knowledge and the speed of the transfer and imitation of organizational capabilities: An empirical test. *Organization Science, 6,* 76-92.

Author Index

Subject Index

About the Authors

Steven W. Floyd is Associate Professor and Lawrence J. Ackerman Scholar of Management at the University of Connecticut, where he teaches strategic management and organization theory. Since his graduation from the University of Colorado, his research interests have centered on strategy-making processes, including strategic roles, consensus, involvement, and more recently, strategic renewal. His articles on these and related topics have been published in such journals as the *Academy of Management Review, Strategic Management Journal, Academy of Management Journal, Journal of Management, Academy of Management Executive, Journal of Management Studies,* and *European Journal of Management.* With Bill Wooldridge, he is also the author of a book, titled *The Strategic Middle Manager.* In addition to strategic behavior, Floyd studies the processes associated with corporate entrepreneurship and technological innovation, and research in this domain has been published in *Entrepreneurship: Theory and Practice, Journal of Management Information Systems,* and *Technology Analysis and Strategic Management.* He is a frequent participant in the meetings of the Academy of Management and Strategic Management Society. He and his wife Beverly live in East Haddam, Connecticut, where he enjoys sailboarding and mountain biking.

Bill Wooldridge is Associate Professor of Strategic Management in the Isenberg School of Management at the University of Massachusetts, Amherst. He earned his BS at Ithaca College, and MBA and PhD degrees at the University of Colorado, Boulder. His research with Steven Floyd on the involvement and contributions of mid-level professionals to strategy has appeared in *Strategic Management Journal, Journal of Management Studies, Academy of Management Executive,* and *Entrepreneurship: Theory and Practice.* This research has been cited by the *Economist* and was the basis for a previous book, *The Strategic Middle Manager.* More recently, he has turned his attention to motors of change and their application to competition in the U.S. bicycle industry. An avid cyclist, Bill resides in Belchertown, Massachusetts, with his wife Linda and their children Jenna and Andrew. In his free time, he participates in both recreational and competitive cycling and can often be found at bicycling events around the country.